Active Learning in Secondary and College Science Classrooms

A Working Model for Helping the Learner to Learn

CENTER FOR TEACHING EXCELLENCE
Canisius College

Active Learning in Secondary and College Science Classrooms

A Working Model for Helping the Learner to Learn

Joel A. Michael
Rush Medical College

Harold I. Modell
Physiology Educational Research Consortium

LAWRENCE ERLBAUM ASSOCIATES, PUBLISHERS
2003   Mahwah, New Jersey   London

Lawrence Erlbaum Associates, Inc., Publishers
10 Industrial Avenue
Mahwah, NJ 07430

Cover design by Kathryn Houghtaling Lacey

Library of Congress Cataloging-in-Publication Data

Michael, Joel A., 1940-
    Active learning in secondary and college science classrooms: a working model for helping the learner to learn / Joel A. Michael, Harold I. Modell.
        p. cm.
    Includes bibliographical references and index.
    ISBN 0-8058-3947-X (acid-free paper)
    ISBN 0-8058-3948-8 (pbk. : acid-free paper)
    1. Science—Study and teaching (Secondary) 2. Science—Study and teaching (Higher) I. Modell, Harold I. II. Title.

Q181.M46 2003
507'.1—dc21   2003040769
                                                                          CIP

Books published by Lawrence Erlbaum Associates are printed on acid-free paper, and their bindings are chosen for strength and durability.

Printed in the United States of America
10   9   8   7   6   5   4   3   2   1

This book is dedicated to our students, past, present, and future. They have provided us, and we expect, will continue to provide us, with the challenges and rewards that make our careers exciting and fulfilling.

CONTENTS

     Collaborative Learning

Part IV: Assessment in an Active Learning Environment

12   Assessment of Student Performance   117
13   How Do I Know It's Working?   127
14   The Teacher as a Reflective Practitioner   137

Part V: Summing Up

15   The Challenges of Helping the Learner to Learn   143
16   Building a Community of Active Learning Practitioners   153
17   The Bottom Line   157

     References   159

     Author Index   165

     Subject Index   169

PREFACE

This book is about "helping the learner to learn." While this phrase seems to merely describe what all good teachers strive to do, it really describes something more than that. This phrase should be understood as a short-hand description of a *mindset* that directs all aspects of the teacher's behavior. Our purpose is to help you, the reader, to reflect on the implications of what it means to help the learner to learn and to think about what this might mean in very concrete ways in a variety of educational settings.

The working model we present in this book is relevant to any teaching context. However, our focus here is on teaching in secondary and college science classrooms. Within this context, our specific goals are:

- To help science faculty examine and redefine their roles in the classroom;
- To define for secondary and college science teachers in all disciplines a framework for thinking about active learning and the creation of an active learning environment; and
- To provide science faculty with the assistance they need to begin building successful active learning environments in their classrooms.

Our assumption is that you are reading this book because you have already decided to look for ways to change how you teach, or that you are, at the very least, prepared to think about doing this. For those of you who are still preparing to teach, our aim is to help you think about how you will teach when you finally find yourself in the classroom.

To reach our goal of helping you adopt a new approach to teaching, we will take you on a journey on which you will find exposition, opportunities for exploration, and chances for reflection.

We have organized this book into five sections.

In Part I (Building the Foundation for an Approach to Active Learning), we will first consider what we know about learning (chap. 1) and then discuss what is meant by "meaningful learning" (chap. 2). We then propose a simple model for the educational process (chap. 3) that we will use to structure the remainder of our journey.

In Part II (Roles for the Teacher in Creating an Active Learning Environment), we consider the roles of the teacher as described by our model: defining the students' expected output state (chap. 4), determining the students' input state (chap. 5), and creating the learning experiences that make up a course (chap. 6).

We then turn from the general to the specific, and, in Part III (Creating Active Learning Environments), we describe what one must do to create an active learning environment in the classroom. Chapter 7 deals with the issue of preparing students to participate in an active learning environment. Chapters 8, 9, and 10 discuss ideas associated with promoting active learning in lecture, discussion, and laboratory settings. Chapter 11 discusses cooperative and collaborative learning, newer approaches to science learning.

In Part IV (Assessment in an Active Learning Environment), we deal with questions about what is really happening in the active learning environment you create: Chapter 12 discusses evaluating student performance. Chapter 13 raises the issue of how you can know if your efforts to promote active learning are working, and Chapter 14 discusses the idea that the teacher must be a reflective practitioner.

Finally, we bring our journey to a close in Part V (Summing Up). Chapter 15 presents a frank discussion of the challenges that you may encounter in attempting to change the way you teach. Chapter 16 describes the process of building an academic community of active learning practitioners. We end in Chapter 17 with a review of our "take home" messages.

We have brought a perspective to the task of writing this book that, if not unique, is relatively uncommon. Both authors were trained as physiologists in graduate programs at major research universities. We began our academic careers at institutions that, nevertheless, expected us to *teach* as well as do research. Both of us became heavily involved with educational issues as a result of our individual work in computer-based education in physiology. We approached our roles in the classroom in much the same way as we functioned in the laboratory, asking questions, observing outcomes, and trying new approaches to reach our goal of enabling student learning. At different times and for different reasons, we both abandoned our physiology research programs to devote full time to research and faculty development activities in science education. Thus, we bring our experiences as scientists (in both physiology and education), as classroom teachers (at a variety of post-secondary levels), and as experienced faculty development practitioners to this book.

ACKNOWLEDGMENTS

The ideas in this book are the product of more than 10 years of research and a nearly non-stop dialogue about learning and teaching. We are indebted to our colleagues in the Physiology Educational Research Consortium, and especially Allen Rovick and Mary Pat Wenderoth, for their vigorous participation in this dialogue and for their many insights. We would also like to thank the National Institutes of Health, the Office of Naval Research, and the National Science Foundation for their support of our research efforts in this area. (This project was supported, in part, by NSF grant number REC-9909411.)

Joel Michael would like to express his appreciation for the support that he has received over the years from his wife, Greta. She has been an important sounding board for ideas and a marvelous proofreader when that has been needed. He also wishes to acknowledge his daughters, Jennifer and Erica. He learned a great deal about teaching and learning from watching their progress through many years of school.

Harold Modell appreciates the role that his wife, Jane, plays as a life partner and best friend. She always offers encouragement and support when it is needed most. He also offers thanks to his daughter, Tamara, who has participated as a colleague in the development process that has led to recognizing the power of the "helping the learner to learn mindset."

—Joel Michael
—Harold Modell

Part I

Building the Foundation
for an Approach to Active Learning

Chapter

1

What Is Learning and How Does It Occur?

CHAPTER OVERVIEW

Learning is a change in behavior that results from the learner's interaction with the environment (experience). Recent advances in cognitive science are beginning to provide us with some general principles, applicable in education, that should facilitate learning. (1) All learning occurs on the foundation of already learned knowledge and skills. (2) To the extent that the old knowledge is faulty, the learning of new knowledge will be compromised. (3) Declarative (what) and procedural (how) knowledge are different, and the processes of learning them are different. (4) Learning declarative knowledge involves building mental representations or models. (5) Practice with timely and appropriate feedback is required for all procedural learning. (6) Retention and the ability to utilize knowledge (meaningful learning) is facilitated by building connections (links) between old knowledge structures and the new knowledge being learned. (7) The ability to construct multiple representations of the new knowledge is an important component of meaningful learning. (8) Some knowledge and skills, when acquired, are context-specific while other knowledge and skills may be more readily transferred to a new domain. (9) Collaborative or cooperative effort can yield more individual learning than individual effort alone. (10) Articulating explanations, whether to peers, teachers, or one's self, facilitates learning.

Examples of learning are all around us. The neighbors' new baby is learning to speak Hindi from its grandmother. Your brother's baby is learning to walk. Your daughter has learned to ride a two-wheeled bicycle. Your son has learned all the presidents in chronological order. Your sister has gone back to school and is learning to be a lawyer. Your spouse has learned to use a

3

spreadsheet at work, and you have learned to use a database program to keep track of your collection of CDs. Grandma has learned to use e-mail to keep in touch with all her grandchildren.

BEFORE PROCEEDING!

Think about something that you recently learned to do (NOT some fact that you recently acquired). How did you learn whatever you learned? What steps did you have to go through? How did you know when you had succeeded?

What, if anything, do all of these examples of "learning" have in common? In each instance, some observable, more or less permanent change in the learner's behavior has occurred as a result of his or her interaction with a particular environment. Learning is the result of experience. This is nothing more than a re-statement of the usual dictionary definition of learning. Nevertheless, such a definition has significant implications for teaching and what happens, or should happen, in the classroom.

This book focuses on how to create a learning environment that will facilitate students' mastery of science. The starting point for such an effort must be an understanding of the processes involved in learning. The next step, and it is an essential one, is for teachers to redefine their roles in the classroom. This will be a recurring theme throughout this book.

WHAT DO WE KNOW ABOUT LEARNING?

Psychology has studied learning and the related phenomenon of memory since the late 19th century. The development of cognitive science and its multiple-disciplinary approach to such questions has hastened the pace of these studies enormously over the past 40 years. *Cognitive Science*, one of the premier journals of this discipline, bills itself as "A Multidisciplinary Journal of Artificial Intelligence, Linguistics, Neuroscience, Philosophy, Psychology." Controversies abound in learning research about issues of experimental methodology, interpretation of data, and even what questions can be asked and potentially answered. Nevertheless, it is possible to summarize what we have learned about learning. The set of assertions that follow can serve to guide you as you plan and implement the learning environment in which your students will function.

One of the dominant schools of thought about learning, one that is particularly prevalent in all discussions of science learning, is **constructivism**.

The constructivist approach to learning had one point of origin in the work of Piaget and his followers and another in the information processing paradigm that came to be prominent in cognitive science. There are now many different forms of constructivism, but each of them embraces several basic tenets. First, knowledge cannot be ***transmitted*** from one individual to another individual in any mode. Knowledge is ***built*** by the learner using internal cognitive processes acting on stimuli from the environment. The result is a mental representation, or model, of the "real world" that can be used to solve problems. These representations or models may be well defined or they may be ill defined. In any event, as the learner continues to learn, they will be modified and refined.

Of course, this means that it is the **learner** who is responsible for the learning that occurs. It also means that all we, as teachers, can do is to help the learner to learn. Second, the learner's process of building new knowledge starts with a foundation of everything that is already known by the learner. The learner is *not* simply a blank slate (*tabula rasa*) on which experience writes the new lessons being learned (Bransford, Brown, & Cocking, 1999).

It is clear, however, that at least some of what the learner already "knows" is wrong in whole or in part. This "wrong" knowledge has been labeled by investigators as misconceptions, alternative conceptions, and naive theories (Wandersee, Mintzes, & Novak, 1994). Whatever labels are used, they describe some kind of conceptual difficulty that the student is having (Michael et al., 2002). We will use the term *misconceptions* to refer to such "incorrect" knowledge. The significance of misconceptions is that their presence inevitably interferes with the learner's attempt to incorporate new, correct knowledge that is to be learned into that which is already known. Learning requires "repair" of existing mental representations (models) to correct misconceptions while simultaneously extending the model to include new concepts. Thus, learning is often talked about as representing a process of "conceptual change" (Smith, 1991).

In thinking about learning, it is important to recognize that there are at least three different kinds of "things" that can be learned: (1) declarative knowledge, (2) procedural knowledge, and (3) psychomotor skills. As we will see, all three have been extensively studied by the learning sciences.

Declarative knowledge is the "what" of a particular topic. It can be a set of facts that defines aspects of the subject matter. The facts can be as simple as the *definition of terms* ("amino acids are … ," "the resting potential is … ," "igneous rock is … ") or a collection of *data* ("normal mean arterial pressure is … ," "the equilibrium constant for this reaction is … ," "the value of the gravitational constant is … "). Declarative knowledge can also be more complex and consist of *concepts* (osmotic pressure, host defense, plate tectonics), *general principles* (conservation of mass), or defined *relationships* between entities (cardiac output equals stroke volume times heart rate, an increase in the population of predators will lead to a decrease in the population of prey).

Declarative knowledge is stored as mental representations or mental models. Although there are a number of competing theories describing these mental "entities," the idea that new declarative knowledge must be related to (connected to, linked to) the knowledge already present is universally accepted. The richer the links, the better the new knowledge will be retained, and the more readily the knowledge can be retrieved for use in problem solving (see chap. 2).

In other words, learning involves the process of building mental models from existing and new information and testing these models. We will define learning in the context of helping the learner to learn as the iterative process of building, testing, and refining mental models (see Figure 1.1). We define an *active learning environment* as one in which students are engaged in the process of building, testing, and refining their mental models.

Rote learning ("memorizing") of declarative knowledge is a common component of all school-based learning. Learning the elements in the periodic table by repeated recitation and correction is a clear example of rote learning. Experimental psychology has studied memorization tasks like this for many years, and we have a good understanding of the factors that determine the success or failure of memorizing. However, it is generally agreed that rote learning is a low-level cognitive process that can only provide information ("facts") that may or may not be used later for higher levels of learning. Our interest, one that is shared by most teachers, is in helping students accomplish meaningful learning in which facts are accumulated and *organized* into a conceptual framework, or mental model, that allows these "facts" to be used to accomplish tasks in the real world (see chap. 2).

LEARNING is
BUILDING,
TESTING, and
REFINING
MENTAL MODELS

FIG. 1.1. One definition of learning.

Procedural knowledge deals with "how" to do certain things. A student can memorize the multiplication table in a rote manner, thus acquiring some body of declarative knowledge. However, multiplication of two 2-digit numbers requires the student to learn a **procedure** that will use the memorized multiplication table in a certain sequence of actions to accomplish the assigned task. Practice using procedures is essential, as is the availability of timely and appropriate feedback about the success or failure of the process. After sufficient practice, the procedure being learned becomes essentially automatic, and the individual may no longer find it easy to articulate the steps that he or she applied in carrying out the process. Problem solving of any sort requires a library of procedural knowledge that can be drawn upon as needed.

There are several steps in the process of acquiring procedural knowledge. The learner must first understand what the task is, then master the individual, basic steps in the process and, finally, must become proficient at performing the task. Learning procedures requires opportunities for practice. However, mere repetition of the task does not necessarily result in proficiency. An essential element is feedback that informs the learner about what was done right and what was not. This feedback is analogous to the model testing just described for declarative knowledge.

For example, to solve physics problems requires identifying what is being asked (what's the problem), identifying the major laws (concepts) that must be employed to reach a solution, deciding on the appropriate mathematical representation of the law, representing the forces acting on the system, and finally correctly manipulating the equations that are being used. This procedure for solving physics problems must be practiced if the learner is to become proficient at it. But the feedback provided to the learner must go beyond simply identifying an answer as right or wrong, or simply providing an example of a correct solution. Each of the steps must be critiqued, and the learner must be helped to understand which steps were done correctly and which were not.

Psychomotor skills refer to the ability to do things in the physical world. Learning to ride a two-wheeled bicycle is an example of acquiring a psychomotor skill. So, too, is learning to use a microscope (focusing, moving the stage to find a structure on the slide). Other examples include learning to dissect a frog or manipulating a computer-based data acquisition system in the physics laboratory. We must note that acquiring some psychomotor skills requires no declarative knowledge and only a little procedural knowledge. For example, it is of little use to "tell" a child how to ride a bicycle. On the other hand, learning to dissect a frog is a psychomotor skill, one that requires the coordination of declarative ("the heart is located in ... ") and procedural knowledge ("first, cut the skin above ... ") as well as the acquisition of the required motor skills.

We must emphasize that learning is almost always an iterative process. Building appropriate mental models of "science phenomena" requires repeated hypothesis testing and, based on experimental data, revising of the model being tested. The same is true for procedural knowledge. Learning to play a musical instrument, learning to solve a class of problems, or becoming proficient at performing a laboratory task requires doing the task, analyzing the performance, and making adjustments before repeating the task.

MEANINGFUL LEARNING

Bloom (1956), in his now famous, or perhaps infamous, *Taxonomy of Educational Objectives* defines a range of behaviors that reflects different levels of learning. At the bottom is "rote" learning. However, it is widely acknowledged that education should help the learner to develop higher levels of learning, sometimes referred to as learning with understanding or ***meaningful learning***. Regardless of which term you use, the implications include the ability to use or apply knowledge to solve problems. This requires that acquired knowledge (declarative and procedural) be more or less easily retrieved, and that the learner has the skills needed to solve problems. There is evidence that meaningful learning is associated with a rich network of links or connections between new and old knowledge. When meaningful learning has occurred, the learner is likely to possess multiple representations of the knowledge and skills obtained, and she or he has the ability to pick the model that most usefully supports the problem-solving process being exercised (chap. 2).

An important aspect of meaningful learning in any domain is the extent to which what has been learned can be applied in, or transferred to, a context, or even a domain, different from the one in which it was originally learned. It is clear that some learning is very domain specific with little or no transfer out of the original domain. Understanding kinematics, an important topic in physics, and being able to solve problems about the motion of objects, does not transfer to an understanding of AC electrical circuits, an equally important topic in physics. In many domains the processes to be learned to solve problems are specific to that domain or set of problems. Knowing how to solve physics problems does not enable one to balance chemical equations.

However, there are general problem-solving strategies that can be learned that make one a better problem solver in many different domains. Furthermore, there are skills with which learners (the problem solver) can monitor their own problem-solving process (think about their own thinking). These skills are often referred to as metacognition, and mastery of metacognitive skills should be a goal of all education.

The "richness" of the context in which learning occurs (the extent to which it relates to the learner's past experiences, the complexity of the situation and the extent to which a wide array of past learning is relevant) seems to affect the learning that occurs. The richer the learning context the more opportunity the learner will have to link or associate what he is learning with knowledge and skills he has already mastered. One way in which the richness of the learning context can be increased is to encourage the learner to elaborate, expand, and, in more general terms, generate his or her own explanation for the new knowledge or skills being acquired. This "self-explanation" effect has been studied extensively, and the benefits have been clearly established (Chi, DeLeeuw, Chiu, & LaVancher, 1994). Another way in which this same effect can be realized is for the learner to simultaneously act as a teacher ("the best way to learn something is to teach it"), since teaching requires the generation of explanations, both for oneself and for the learner (see chap. 11 in particular).

Several seemingly disparate strands of research in cognitive science and education lead to the suggestion that students working together in groups may learn more than students working individually. Studies from developmental psychology, the sociology of science as a group process, examination of classroom conversation, and a growing movement within cognitive science that emphasizes the social construction of knowledge, all support the positive influence of students working together. The value of cooperative or collaborative learning (see chap. 11), peer teaching or tutoring, and reciprocal teaching arise, at least in part, from the creation of a learning environment in which explanation and self-explanation are fostered.

THE EDUCATIONAL IMPLICATIONS
OF OUR UNDERSTANDING OF LEARNING

Ten key ideas about learning (see Table 1.1) emerge from the preceding discussion. In the remainder of this chapter, we will point out the educational implications of each of them as they relate to your task of helping the learner to learn. The remainder of the book will build on these assertions as we proceed to discuss science learning and teaching.

Key Idea 1: All Learning Occurs on the Foundation of Already Learned Knowledge and Skills.

A student entering the classroom is *not* a *tabula rasa*. The new material being learned will be "written on the slate" along with, or perhaps over, what-

TABLE 1.1
Key ideas about learning

- All learning occurs on the foundation of already learned knowledge and skills.
- To the extent that the old knowledge is faulty, the learning of new knowledge will be compromised.
- Declarative (what) and procedural (how) knowledge are different and the processes of learning them are different.
- Learning declarative knowledge involves building mental models or representations.
- Practice with timely and appropriate feedback is required for all procedural learning.
- Retention and the ability to utilize knowledge (meaningful learning) are facilitated by building connections (links) between old knowledge structures and the new knowledge being learned.
- The ability to construct multiple representations of new knowledge is an important component of meaningful learning.
- Some knowledge and skills, when acquired, are context-specific while other knowledge and skills may be more readily transferred to a new domain.
- Collaborative or cooperative effort can yield more individual learning than individual effort alone.
- Articulating explanations, whether to peers, teachers, or one's self, facilitates learning.

ever is already there. Furthermore, what is already there cannot be ignored by the learner. Old knowledge will be incorporated into, or related to, whatever is being newly learned. This is perhaps the major tenet of constructivism, still the dominant theoretical approach to understanding learning, especially in the sciences (Appleton, 1997).

Every student, every learner, "knows" something about the topic to be learned. However, he or she may not realize this initially and may even deny it. This "knowledge" may come from the individual's personal experience in the physical world, through interactions with parents, siblings and friends, from the media, from the very language we use, and, of course, from previous schooling. Some of this prior knowledge is correct; some of it is correct but incomplete; some is only partially correct; and some of it is simply wrong. Nevertheless, all attempts to learn something new will be built on the foundations provided by that old "knowledge," right or wrong.

Educational Implications. There are several implications of this tenet about learning. First, it is essential that you understand what the students already know when they embark on any learning experience. Without an understanding of the input state of the students (see chap. 5 for a broad discussion of the notion of the input state), it is impossible for you to set realistic goals for your students and impossible to plan activities that will help the students reach those goals.

Second, it is essential that you understand that some of what the students bring to the classroom is flawed (incomplete or simply wrong). One goal for all teachers is presumably to help students correct existing mental models. Without knowing what misconceptions are prevalent, it is impossible for you to plan activities that will help students correct their mental models. Another goal must be to avoid inadvertently contributing to the students' building faulty mental models because of something that happens in your classroom.

Finally, since new knowledge will be learned in the context of old knowledge, it is important for the teacher to understand the students' prior knowledge so that new material can be organized and presented in a way that can be most appropriately related to the old knowledge

Key Idea 2: To the Extent That the Old Knowledge Is Faulty, the Learning of New Knowledge Will Be Compromised.

The terms misconceptions, preconceptions, alternative conceptions, and naive conceptions have been used to describe this faulty knowledge (Wandersee et al., 1994). While these terms are not synonymous, we can say that each refers to aspects of existing mental models that are at variance with accepted scientific knowledge (even when the faulty mental model has some demonstrable utility in the student's life). Since all learning occurs by building new knowledge on top of the foundation of old knowledge, there is clearly a problem to be overcome when some of that old knowledge is wrong. If nothing else, there will be conflicts between the old, faulty model and the correct model that is being built. Misconceptions are known to be deeply entrenched and quite difficult to correct or remediate by the usual teaching strategies.

Educational Implications.   Again, it must be stressed that you need to understand that misconceptions exist, and you need to know what misconceptions your students exhibit. That being said, it is important for you to understand that telling the learner that some piece of their knowledge is wrong, or simply attempting to provide them with, "give" them, the right knowledge, DOES NOT WORK. At most, what will be accomplished by this is that the learner will now store away two different sets of facts or mental models. Which mental model will be used will then depend on the student's perception of which model is appropriate to use in a particular context. In school learners may use one model, and in the "real world," they may use the other model.

Just as students come into the classroom with misconceptions, it is important to recognize that things that happen in the classroom may very well create new misconceptions or at least reinforce old ones, even though that is obviously not your intention. Teachers must be sensitive to the mechanisms that are known to contribute to misconception formation and seek to minimize their occurrence in the classroom. For example, while analogies can be powerful aids to learning, their misuse in the classroom can lead to serious misconceptions if the learner over-generalizes the analogy to situations in which it does not apply (Spiro, Feltovich, Coulson, & Anderson, 1989).

It seems obvious, then, that you must understand what misconceptions your students hold and the possible origins of those faulty models. In Chapter 5, we will discuss ways in which teachers can diagnose the presence of misconceptions, and in Chapters 8 to 11 we will address some specific learning environments in which learners can be assisted in repairing their mental models.

In brief, providing the learner with opportunities for active learning, whether in the lecture hall, discussion section, or student laboratory, can provide opportunities for students to test their own models, discover their shortcomings, and hence, prepare the way for learning the correct model.

Key Idea 3: Declarative (What) and Procedural (How) Knowledge Are Different, and the Processes of Learning Them Are Different.

Students asked to learn Newton's three laws, that is, *memorize* them (acquire declarative knowledge), engage in mental processes that are quite different from the processes they will use if asked to learn to *solve problems* (acquire procedural knowledge) about moving objects.

Educational Implications.   It is important that you understand the difference between declarative and procedural knowledge for several reasons. Your decisions about the learning objectives for some content area in your course must reflect the type of knowledge being addressed; some objectives will involve acquiring declarative knowledge and some will necessitate acquiring procedural knowledge. You must then make learning resources available to facilitate student mastery of both types of knowledge. In addition, your assessments must be appropriate for the kinds of knowledge you have asked the students to learn. If students are expected to master both declarative and procedural knowledge, it is essential that assessment tools test for the mastery of both kinds of knowledge. We will have more to say about assessment in Chapter 12.

Key Idea 4: Learning Declarative Knowledge Involves Building Mental Models or Representations.

Learning generally involves long-term acquisition (storage) of information. Various proposals have been advanced for describing exactly how declarative knowledge is stored (e.g., schemas, scripts, and production rules). Each offers a somewhat different description of the elements that make up the mental representation or model of whatever is being stored. Whatever the nature of the mental representations (models), the new knowledge being acquired will be related in some way to existing models. The new knowledge may be directly incorporated into existing models, or the representation of the new knowledge may be linked to, or associated with, the old, existing models. The ability to generate multiple representations or models of the knowledge being learned, and to connect them to prior knowledge, is both a sign of deep understanding and a powerful tool in solving problems using this knowledge.

Educational Implications. It is essential that the learner be given opportunities to build many different models of the knowledge being learned, perhaps differing in the sensory modality that is activated (vision or audition) or the source of the information that is used. Aids to relating the new knowledge being learned to old knowledge are also helpful. It is also important that learners be required to think about their models in an overt and explicit way. In some instances it may be helpful for the learner to use specific model-building skills such as concept mapping (Novak & Gowin, 1984; Novak, 1998). We will explore different ways to actively engage students in thinking about and using their own mental models (chap. 8–11).

Key Idea 5: Practice With Timely and Appropriate Feedback Is Required for All Procedural and Psychomotor Learning.

There are several steps in the process of learning any skill, whether the skill is a cognitive one (solving a problem) or a psychomotor one (doing something physical). The learner must first understand what it is that he or she is being asked to do (obtain a well-focused image of cell structures at different depths in a thick section, determine the chemical composition of an unknown sample). The learner must then master the individual, basic steps in the process that is involved. Finally, he or she must become proficient at performing the task.

Procedural and psychomotor learning requires opportunities for practice. However, mere repetition of the task does not necessarily result in proficiency. An essential element that must be present in the practice setting is feedback that informs the learner about what was done right and what was not. In attempting to learn procedural or psychomotor skills, students can often benefit from observing such skills being modeled by the teacher.

Educational Implications. Practice and appropriate feedback are the keys to procedural learning. Thus, the learning environment must provide opportunities for students to solve problems or practice some motor skill and receive appropriate, timely feedback. This can be difficult to arrange. Students learning to solve problems need to have access to many problems. Learning to prepare a thin section of a mineral sample for microscopy requires many samples and adequate access to the needed equipment. Moreover, many of the educational experiences commonly incorporated into science courses may not help students reach the desired level of mastery. Textbook problems with their minimalist solutions at the end of the chapter or book may not provide enough feedback to help the learner. Similarly, watching you solve a problem at the board is all too often a passive experience for students, one that contributes little to procedural learning. Watching you carry out a task in the laboratory will not lead to the level of student proficiency desired. In Chapters 2 (problem solving) and 10 (laboratories), we will discuss ways to build learning environments that facilitate the students' mastery of procedural skills.

Key Idea 6: Retention and the Ability to Utilize Knowledge (Meaningful Learning) Is Facilitated by Building Connections (Links) Between Old Knowledge Structures and the New Knowledge Being Learned.

The idea of meaningful learning, or learning with understanding, is meant to denote the acquisition of knowledge in a way that allows it to be accessed when needed and makes it possible to be used to solve problems (chap. 2). Constructivism asserts that it is the mental activity of the learner that builds mental models (representations) of the new knowledge on top of, or connected to, previously learned knowledge. The more links or connections between the new and old, the more firmly the new knowledge will be **retained**. Furthermore, the more links that are available, the more likely it is that a piece of information can be **retrieved** when it is needed to solve a problem. The more links or connections that are present, the more likely it is that some feature of a problem being solved will activate the retrieval of the needed knowledge so that the student can **do** something with it.

Educational Implications. In order for you to assist students to link their new knowledge to their old knowledge, it is essential that you have some idea of what is in the students' existing knowledge base. Knowing this, you can assist students to overtly and explicitly build links or associations with that old knowledge. Furthermore, having insight into the students' old knowledge base helps you put the new material into a context that students are likely to find most relevant and, thus, more easily related to their old knowledge.

Key Idea 7: The Ability to Construct Multiple Representations of New Knowledge Is an Important Component of Meaningful Learning.

Meaningful learning is universally taken to be the goal of all education. This refers to the state in which the new material being learned is related to, or incorporated into, existing mental representations (models) of already learned material. When meaningful learning has occurred, when the learner's mental representations of knowledge are richly interconnected, both retention and retrieval of knowledge are facilitated. With richly linked mental models, the learner is better able to use his or her knowledge and skills to solve problems never before encountered. Unlike that which has been learned by rote and is more or less "inert," that which has been learned in a meaningful way can be used.

Furthermore, it appears that building multiple representations of the new knowledge contributes significantly to the learner's ability to use that knowledge to solve problems. For example, a student learning about the cardiovascular system will benefit from being able to construct models at the cell level (the cardiac muscle cell), the anatomical level (the structure of the heart and circulation), as well as the functional level (the physiology of the heart and circulation). Studies of expert vs. novice problem-solvers in domains such as physics reveal that the expert can categorize the problem to be solved in a number of different ways; i.e., the expert has multiple models with which to think about the problem. Solving the problem thus begins with selecting the most appropriate model for the task at hand.

Educational Implications. All learning environments must provide the learner with opportunities to engage new material in a context that facilitates establishing relationships between the old and the new. Further, the learning environment must make obvious the relationships that exist between what the learner already knows and what he or she is attempting to learn.

Success at meaningful learning will be facilitated if the learner is given opportunities to create multiple representations of the new knowledge being acquired. One way to do this is to provide new information using multiple modalities (vision, audition, touch). Another useful tactic is to provide different examples of the phenomenon being learned, thus facilitating links to many different, already stored mental models.

Key Idea 8: Some Knowledge and Skills, When Acquired, Are Context-Specific While Other Knowledge and Skills May Be More Readily Transferred to a New Domain.

A student who has acquired skill in solving algebra word problems cannot necessarily solve physics problems (which requires an ability to analyze the forces that are acting on the system in addition to being able perform the needed algebraic manipulation of the relevant equations), and the ability to solve a physics problem does not mean that the student can solve a chemistry problem (balancing a chemical equation requires a knowledge of stoichiometry). The skills that are required for carrying out each of these three examples of problem solving do not transfer between disciplines.

However, a student who understands pressure and flow relationships in the cardiovascular system should be able to use that understanding to solve a problem about air flow in the respiratory system. Algebra, once learned, should be applicable wherever appropriate equations are encountered, and the ability to balance a chemical equation, learned in a chemistry course, should be applicable when dealing with a biology or geology topic. Of course, students are not always able to demonstrate the transfer that we expect. Nevertheless, the goal of meaningful learning specifically addresses this issue of transfer or generality. The better something is learned or understood, the more readily it can be applied to new topics.

Educational Implications. If certain skills can be generalized, and if certain scientific models can be applied to many situations, it is imperative that students be taught these skills and models. Furthermore, you must help students become aware of the general nature of these skills and models and recognize situations in which they apply. This focus on generality must start with the initial learning and must be reinforced as each new opportunity for application is encountered.

Key Idea 9: Collaborative or Cooperative Effort Can Yield More Individual Learning Than Individual Effort Alone.

Small group learning environments have been incorporated into the curriculum in a great many ways and with the intention of realizing a number of different ends. Collaborative or cooperative learning groups are examples of such learning environments (Bossert, 1988; Goodsell, Maher, & Tinto, 1992; Watson, 1992). Small group problem-solving sessions provide yet another environment in which students are encouraged to work together (Michael & Rovick, 1999). Although it can be argued that collaborative and cooperative work are NOT the same thing, our focus is on the use of small-group, interactive learning environments of all kinds (chap. 11), and we would argue that the common features that make both collaborative and cooperative learning effective (involving students learning with other students) overshadow the differences between them.

There is considerable evidence from studies of different "collaborative" learning settings that students working together each individually learn more than students working alone (Lunetta, 1990).

Educational Implications. Collaborative or cooperative learning environments, as is the case for any active learning environment (see chap. 8–11), provide the teacher with opportunities to interact with students in a manner that is profitable to both teacher and students. You will be better able to diagnose students' misconceptions and learning difficulties (chap. 5). Students can more readily obtain the feedback they need to learn the skills involved in applying their growing knowledge. These learning environments also require students to articulate their understanding or explain their reasoning to one another, and thereby help each of them to build robust mental models (engage in meaningful learning).

Key Idea 10: Articulating Explanations, Whether to Peers, Teachers, or One's Self, Facilitates Learning.

All too often, learning is treated as though it should literally be a silent process with the learner reading or listening or perhaps solving a problem. However, there is considerable evidence that when learners are required to articulate their current understanding of the material (either to themselves, their peers, or their instructors), learning is facilitated.

Educational Implications. The benefit to students of having to articulate their knowledge is one explanation for the benefits of collaborative/cooperative learning. In all settings in which students work together to learn or solve a problem, one critical feature is the need for the learners to communicate with one another. Communication is essential if information is to be shared and ideas exchanged. Arguing and debating issues, negotiating and reaching agreements in order to complete the assigned task, all require that each individual be able to articulate to others what he or she believes, understands, and doesn't understand. When learners who are solving problems generate explanations of what they are doing, whether voiced or not, they seem to learn more. Clearly, then, you need to create learning environments in which students are encouraged to talk to students and to you.

WHERE DO WE GO FROM HERE? INCORPORATING THESE IDEAS ABOUT LEARNING INTO YOUR TEACHING

Constructivism has demonstrated great explanatory power about what happens in our classrooms. While it does not answer all of the questions about learning and certainly does not provide a prescription for what we ought to do in the classroom, it does offer solid evidence in support of many things that the supporters of active learning have always done in the classroom.

Our intention in providing this synopsis of current learning theory is to make it easier for you to begin applying these ideas in a more deliberate, self-conscious manner. The Suggested Readings at the end of this chapter list several sources that provide more complete treatments of contemporary learning theory.

Our goal in this book is to help you begin thinking in a different way about what you do in the classroom. We hope to help you redefine your job there and the approach you take to interacting with your students. A first step is understanding how learning occurs.

SUGGESTED READINGS

Anderson, J. R. (1995). *Cognitive psychology and its implications* (4th edition). New York: W. H. Freeman.

Bransford, J. D., Brown, A. L., & Cocking, R. R. (Eds.). (1999). *How people learn: Brain, mind, experience, and school.* Washington, DC: National Academy Press.

Gabel, D. L. (Ed.). (1994). *Handbook of research on science teaching and learning.* New York: Macmillan Publishing Company.

Gardner, M., Greeno, J. G., Reif, F., Schoenfeld, A. H., diSessa, A., & Stage, E. (Eds). (1990). *Towards a scientific practice of science education.* Hillsdale, NJ: Lawrence Erlbaum Associates.

Glynn, S. M., Yeany, R. H., & Britton, B. K. (Eds.). (1991). *The psychology of learning science.* Hillsdale, NJ: Lawrence Erlbaum Associates.

Goodsell, A., Maher, M., & Tinto, V. (1992). *Collaborative learning: a sourcebook for higher education.* University Park, PA: National Center for Postsecondary Teaching, Learning, and Assessment.

Reigeluth, C. M. (Ed.). (1999). *Instructional-design theories and models, Volume II: A new paradigm of instructional theory.* Hillsdale, NJ: Lawrence Erlbaum Associates.

Chapter

2

Meaningful Learning
and Problem Solving in Science

CHAPTER OVERVIEW

Learning with understanding (meaningful learning) is universally acknowledged to be one goal of science education. The most immediate "test" of understanding is whether the learner can "do something" with what has been learned. In the sciences, solving problems is one such test of understanding. Problem solving is what one does when the answer to a question or the solution to a problem cannot simply be retrieved from memory. Relevant information must be identified or obtained (from memory or from external sources), and something must be done with the information (compare, contrast, integrate, calculate, etc.) to arrive at the desired end state (answer or solution). In the sciences, students are expected to solve a variety of problems. Problems may be qualitative (predict whether something will increase, decrease, or remain unchanged), quantitative (calculate something), or may require generating an explanation for some phenomenon or observation.

In Chapter 1, we defined the learning that we want to help students accomplish as the iterative process of building, testing, and refining mental models. The goal that most instructors would set for this learning is to help students "understand" science. This means that we want students to go beyond merely memorizing science "facts" and be able to use the knowledge that they have acquired to solve science-related problems. In other words, students should be able to "use" the knowledge they have gained in novel situations, ones that they have not previously encountered. This, of course, requires students to "know" many "facts," be able to organize those facts into concepts, relate these concepts to other facts and concepts, and know which concepts are relevant to use in dealing with a new situation.

MEANINGFUL LEARNING IS LEARNING
WITH UNDERSTANDING

The ability to "use" knowledge is what is meant by "learning with under-standing" or "meaningful learning," two terms that have become quite common in the education and educational research literature. Learning with understanding (meaningful learning) is universally acknowledged to be one of the major, but not exclusive, goals of science education.

Meaningful learning is often contrasted with rote learning, the act of memorizing information with no overt attempt to organize the memorized information or to integrate it into what the learner already knows. Meaningful learning is known to lead to better and longer retention of the newly acquired information. When meaningful learning has occurred, the newly acquired information is more tightly linked to, or related to, old knowledge already in use by the learner. The integration of "new" information and "old" knowledge is one reason retention is better. Such integration of the "new" with the "old" also accounts, in part, for the greater ease with which the "new" information can be retrieved, and, therefore, can be used (see below).

BEFORE PROCEEDING!

What do *you* mean when you ask your students to "understand" some topic from your discipline? How will *your students* know when they have succeeded? How will *you* know when they have succeeded?

Faculty often say that they want their students to "understand" science. However, when asked what students must do to demonstrate that they "understand" something, faculty struggle to explain how they determine if "understanding" has occurred. If we are to help students learn with understanding, we need to examine how "understanding" is viewed and to agree on a definition of "understanding" in the context of helping the learner to learn.

Attempts by cognitive psychologists to define what is meant by "understanding" has focused on two seemingly different, but actually closely related, ideas (Smith, 1991). One can define understanding as the possession of well-structured and interconnected mental representations of the topic to be understood. Alternatively, understanding has been defined in terms of performance, the students' ability to do "useful" things with the information they have acquired. However, in an important sense, both approaches claim that the most immediate "test" of understanding is whether the learner can readily retrieve the learned information when needed and can then use that information to accomplish some task.

Understanding also implies that the learner can use the understood information in a context other than the one in which the information was learned. This ability to transfer what has been learned to novel situations and to use that understanding to accomplish something in the new context seems to correspond to the common sense use of the term "understand."

In the context of our discussions related to helping the learner to learn, understanding is demonstrated when the student is able to predict what will happen in a particular system when the system is perturbed *and* provide an appropriate explanation for the prediction.

PROBLEM SOLVING AND MEANINGFUL LEARNING

In the sciences, solving problems is seen as one test of understanding. Stewart and Hafner (1994) assert that "[u]nderstanding and problem solving are cognitively similar activities." There are various definitions of what a "problem" is and what "problem solving" consists of. All these definitions emphasize the fact that the individual we are talking about (the problem solver) starts in a particular state, wants to get to a different state, and cannot get there by simply retrieving some information from memory. Relevant information must first be identified, and then obtained (from memory or from external sources). Something must then be done with the information (compare, contrast, integrate, calculate, etc.) to arrive at the desired end state (answer or solution).

In the sciences, students are expected to demonstrate their understanding of the discipline by solving a variety of different kinds of problems (Michael & Rovick, 1999). "Textbook problems" may be qualitative (predict the qualitative changes that will occur in the system), quantitative (calculate something), or may require an explanation for some phenomenon or observation (Table 2.1).

TABLE 2.1

Types of problems typically encountered in science courses

Qualitative reasoning problems: Given some change (structural or functional) to a system, or some disturbance applied to the system, predict the changes in function of the system.

Quantitative reasoning problems: Given a description of a system, calculate the value of some variable or variables.

Explain some phenomenon: Provide a description of the causal relationships between variables or components of the system that give rise to the phenomenon to be explained.

Examples of such problems can be found in any science textbook. Obviously, the subject of the problems will depend on the discipline involved, and the complexity of the problems will depend on the academic level of the course for which the textbook is intended. Some examples of problems from chemistry, earth science, and biology are presented in Table 2.2.

"Real world" problems, or cases (see chap. 11), can require students to analyze a situation and apply their understanding to generate an explanation or even a prescription for changing that situation. Examples of "real world" problems from several different disciplines can be found in Table 2.3.

Still another kind of problem solving involves the student applying his or her understanding to actually "doing" science. This can include everything from designing and conducting experiments to analyzing real data to writing a scientific paper (D'Avanzo & McNeal, 1997; Johnson & Raven, 1996; Tortora & Funke, 1997). The goals of such exercises range from motivating learning by capitalizing on student curiosity, to helping students personally build more robust mental models of the phenomena being studied, to helping students learn the scientific method.

Teaching Problem Solving

More than 20 years ago, Donald Norman (1980) observed, "We expect students to solve problems yet seldom teach them about problem solving." Little has changed since then in most classrooms. However, this need not be the case, and there are many examples of approaches to helping students learn the skills needed to solve problems in a particular discipline. These attempts have been aided, at least in part, by progress in understanding how experts and novices (learners) solve problems in their particular disciplines (Lesgold, 1988; Ploger, 1988). Examples of a specific focus on developing student problem solving skills abound in physics (Bagno & Eylon, 1997; Larkin, 1985; Leonard, Dufresne, & Mestre, 1996; Reif, 1985) and chemistry (Bunce, Gabel, & Samuel, 1991; Tsaparlis & Angelopoulos, 2000), and, in physiology, Michael and Rovick (1999) have begun to offer such assistance to students.

There is also much interest in teaching general thinking skills (Halpern, 1996; Segal, Chipman, & Glaser, 1985) that are applicable to all academic disciplines and to the students' lives outside of the classroom. Work in cognitive science has identified general problem-solving algorithms that can be used to solve a large number of different kinds of problems (Simon, 1999).

One important lesson from everyday experience *and* cognitive science research is the need for practice with feedback if a learner is to master a new skill. In this regard, being able to solve problems is no different from being

TABLE 2.2

Examples of questions and problems to be solved from chemistry, earth science, and life science textbooks

Predict whether each of the following substances is more likely to dissolve in carbon tetrachloride, CCl_4, which is non-polar, or in water, which is polar: C_7H_{16}, Na_2SO_4, HCl, I_2.

Calculate the concentration of CO_2 in a soft drink that is bottled with a partial pressure of CO_2 of 4.0 atm over the liquid at 25° C.

Explain why the pressure has an effect on the solubility of O_2 in water but not on the solubility of NaCl in water.

—From Brown, LeMay, and Bursten (2000).

Yakuysk is located in Siberia at about 60 degrees north latitude. This Russian city has one of the highest average annual temperature ranges in the world: 62.2° C (112° F). *Explain* the reasons for the very high annual temperature range.

Speculate on (*"explain"*) the changes in global temperatures that might occur if Earth had substantially more land area and less ocean area than at present. How might such changes influence the biosphere (*"predict"*)?

Mercury is 13 times heavier than water. If you built a barometer using water rather than mercury, how tall would it have to be (*"calculate"*) to record standard sea-level pressure (in centimeters of water)?

Describe (*"predict"*) some of the consequences that a great and prolonged increase in explosive volcanic activity might have on each of the Earth's four spheres.

—From Tarbuck and Lutgens (2000).

Marco tries to hide at the bottom of a swimming hole by breathing in and out through a garden hose that greatly increases his dead space. What happens (*"predict"*) to the following parameters in his arterial blood, and why (*"explain"*)? (a) PCO_2, (b) PO_2, (c) bicarbonation, and (d) pH

If we estimate that total blood volume is 7% of body weight, *calculate* the total blood volume in a 200-lb man and in a 130-lb woman (2.2 lb/kg). What are their plasma volumes (*"calculate"*) if the man's hematocrit is 52% and the woman's hematocrit is 41%?

—From Silverthorn (2000).

Write a paragraph *explaining* why remote islands have a proportionately greater number of indigenous species than do islands close to the mainland.

Mutations can alter the function of an operon; in fact, it was the effects of various mutations that enabled Jacob Monod to figure out how the *lac* operon works. *Predict* how the following mutations would affect *lac* operon function in the presence and absence of allolactose. (a) mutation of regulatory gene so repressor will not bind tp lactose, (b) mutation of operator so repressor will not bind to operator …

—From Campbell, Reece, and Mitchell (1999); emphasis added.

TABLE 2.3

Examples of "real world" problems

Problem solving:

The following is a summary of a newspaper article: "A new treatment for atrial fibrillation due to an excessively rapid rate at the SA node involves a high-voltage electrical pulse administered to the AV node to destroy its autorhythmic cells. A ventricular pacemaker is then implanted in the patient." Briefly explain the physiological rationale for this treatment: Why is a rapid depolarization rate dangerous, why is the AV node destroyed, and why must a pacemaker be implanted?

—From Silverthorn (2001).

Integrative exercises:

Flouridation of drinking water is employed in many places to aid in the prevention of dental caries. Typically the F^- ion concentration is adjusted to about 1 ppb. Some water supplies are also "hard"; that is, they contain certain cations such as Ca^{2+} that interfere with the action of soap. Consider a case where the concentration of Ca^{2+} is 8 ppb. Could a precipitate of CaF_2 form under these conditions? (Make any necessary approximations.)

—From Brown, LeMay and Bursten (2000).

Examining the Earth system:

Hurricanes are among the most severe storms experienced on Earth. When a hurricane makes landfall in the southeastern United Sates what impact might it have on coastal lands, drainage networks (hydrosphere), and natural vegetation (biosphere)?

—From Tarbuck and Lutgens (2000).

able to perform a new dive or a new piano piece. However, this leads to some obvious questions. What constitutes effective practice and how much practice is required? What constitutes effective feedback? When should feedback be offered?

If you want your students to be able solve certain types of problems, then you must provide students with opportunities to solve these problems. Practice **predicting** the changes that will occur in a system will not necessarily translate into proficiency at **explaining** the occurrence of certain phenomena in the system. If you want them to be able to explain things, you have to give them the chance to learn *this* skill. As for how much practice is needed, it clearly depends on the degree of difficulty of the skill you want them to master, as well as the students' starting point ... what they know and can do already. The greater the "distance" they have to go from their starting point, the more practice will be needed; the harder the task, the more practice will be needed; and the more unprepared they are, the more practice that will be needed.

What constitutes effective feedback? The learner needs more than the right answer (common in textbooks) or a copied solution to the problem worked out on the blackboard (as commonly occurs in discussion sections conducted by teaching assistants or even instructors). Basically what the learner requires is a critique of the thinking processes being used (corrections of arithmetic or algebraic errors, while necessary, are never in themselves sufficient). Such a critique can be provided by the teacher who listens to the student explain an answer to a question, or it can be provided by a fellow student (see further). Because not all learning, or problem solving, occurs in class, students also benefit from "model" solutions to problems that focus on the thought process, not just the generation of a correct answer. Michael and Rovick (1999) have provided very detailed descriptions of the answers to their physiology problems and how to think about the problems that include descriptions of the physiological, and where relevant, clinical context for the problem being solved. Brown, LeMay and Bursten (2000) provide similarly worked-out sample chemistry problems, each immediately followed by another practice problem. Gillespie, Humphreys, Baird and Robinson (1986) also provide worked-out examples of chemistry problems, with particular attention given to describing the general approach to be used to solve specific types of problems.

It was just suggested that offering students opportunities to explain their solutions to a problem offers the teacher an opportunity for providing feedback about the students' performance. However, opportunities to articulate their solutions to a problem affords learners another benefit; Chi and her colleagues (Chi & van Lehn, 1991; Chi et al., 1994) have demonstrated quite convincingly that when learners generate their own explanations to the problems they solve, more is learned. This phenomenon may contribute to the benefits seen when students are encouraged to work together solving problems (see further).

There is one other thing that you can do to help students learn to solve problems, you can model the solutions to those problems. If the teacher is like a swim coach, we can say that it helps to see the new dive to be learned demonstrated by an expert. This, however, requires more than mechanically writing out the solution to a quantitative problem on the board or drawing a causal diagram to explain a phenomenon. What is most important is that the students see and hear a step-wise discussion or explanation of how the problem is to be solved.

TWO HEADS ARE BETTER THAN ONE!

That old adage has found considerable support in the educational research literature on cooperative learning (Qin, Johnson, & Johnson, 1995). When students work together in groups to solve problems, there is a significant increase in the learning outcomes (whatever the discipline or the nature of the problem). The benefits of cooperative learning (see chap. 11) are being exploited in all science disciplines. For example, in physics, Heller and her colleagues (Heller & Hollabaugh, 1992; Heller, Keith, & Anderson, 1992) have examined the effects of cooperative learning in both a large introductory physics course at a state university and in a modern physics course in a community college. Jensen and Finley (1996) have shown that students working in pairs to solve problems about evolution exhibit gains in learned outcomes. Dinan and Frydrychowski (1995) found that students working together in groups to learn organic chemistry (with substantial time spent solving problems together) scored better on the final exam than did students learning the same material in a standard lecture format. Doughtery et al. (1995) found a similar effect for students in a general chemistry course. Although many factors must be carefully planned to facilitate the process, cooperative learning was found to lead to superior results for all students compared with solving problems alone.

In this chapter, we have extended our discussion of learning to further clarify our goal for helping the learner to learn. Our goal is to help students engage in meaningful learning. Hence, we expect to help students build mental models that they can use to solve problems. In addition, we have adopted a working definition of understanding. Students demonstrate understanding of a topic when they can make predictions about the system under study and provide appropriate explanations for their predictions. Now that we have our goal in mind, we can begin to discuss how to implement the helping the learner to learn mindset. Our next step is to propose a model that provides an organizational tool for this implementation.

Chapter

3

A Model
for the Learning Environment

CHAPTER OVERVIEW

A simple model, or description, of the learning environment is presented. It consists of three elements—an input state, the educational experience, and an output state. The use of this model in thinking about one's teaching is described.

The instructor's goal in helping the learner to learn is to promote meaningful learning through an iterative process in which students build, test, and refine their mental models. To achieve this goal, we must create an environment in which these processes can occur, and we must design learning experiences that will help students to engage in these learning processes. Our next task, then, is to focus on the learning environment and decide what steps we, as instructors, should take to create an environment in which meaningful learning is most likely to occur.

You interact with students in a variety of settings and in a variety of capacities. You may see students in the lecture hall, student laboratory, small classroom or in your office. You serve as a purveyor of information, as a facilitator, or as an individual tutor. Many instructors view each of these settings and roles as different from one another. However, if your job is to help the learner to learn, the same governing philosophy should guide your interaction with students regardless of the specific setting in which the interaction occurs.

With this in mind, we have adopted a general model of the educational process that serves as a template for our approach to *all* educational activities in which we engage. The model can be seen in Figure 3.1. It consists of three elements—an input state, a learning experience, and an output state.

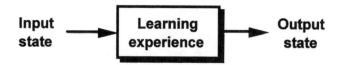

FIG. 3.1. A model of the learning environment.

We can think of these elements as three components of an educational journey. The output state is the destination, where we want the students to get to. The input state is the point of origin, where they are starting out from. The learning experience then is the path over which we guide the students from their point of origin to the destination we have chosen.

Let us briefly examine each of the model's elements and then examine how the model can be applied in a variety of educational settings. We will begin with the output state (the destination), then move to the input state (the origin), and finally examine the learning experiences (route) that help the student make the trip from the input state to the output state.

THE OUTPUT STATE

The output state can be most easily defined as the goal (destination) or set of goals that you establish for each "learning experience." A "learning experience" may be a course, a topic within a course, a discussion within a topic, or a single answer to a student's question. In simple terms, the goal is *what you expect the student to be able to do* upon completing the learning experience. Notice that we did not define this goal solely in terms of information that the student should acquire by the end of the learning experience. If the student has information but cannot use it appropriately, meaningful learning has not occurred, and acquiring the information has been of little value.

The desired output state can fall along a broad spectrum of goals depending on a variety of factors. It might be solving a narrowly focused problem, building a model of a mechanism, solving problems within a topic in a course, or completing all of the learning objectives for the course. Setting an output goal establishes an expectation on the part of the instructor for the performance of the student upon completing the work. The output state defines where the student will be at the end of the particular educational journey we are considering.

THE INPUT STATE

If the output state defines the end of the educational journey, the input state describes the journey's starting point. If your job is to help the learner to learn, it is imperative that you have some idea of the knowledge and skills that the student brings to the educational component as well as the facility with which the student can use that knowledge and those skills. What does the student already know about this topic? How does the student interpret the language or vocabulary associated with the topic or task at hand? What conceptual or reasoning difficulties does the student have with respect to the topic or task at hand?

It is also important to recognize that nonacademic factors contribute to the input state. Does the student's work schedule impact her study time? Does the student's family obligations affect his academic performance? Are the student's cultural beliefs and practices compatible with the learning environment that you envision for your classroom?

In our model, answers to these and similar questions define the "input" state. It is important to recognize that when the educational journey includes a number of intermediate stops, each stop (output state) becomes the point of origin (input state) for the next "leg" of the journey (Fig. 3.2).

Based on past experience and course prerequisites, most instructors make assumptions about the input state of their students, but they seldom test these assumptions. However, as we shall see, these assumptions may not be valid, and, as a result, sufficient information about the input state may not be available. If this is the case, the third element of our model, the learning experience, may not get the students to the chosen destination.

THE LEARNING EXPERIENCE

The learning experience represents the set of activities, classroom experiences, and intellectual challenges that the instructor has designed to help students reach the desired output state. Each experience represents a leg of the route that the student will traverse on his or her journey from the point of origin to the destination. Depending on the students' input state and the desired output state, the learning experience might require students to engage in a debate, solve a particular type of problem, work with a computer simulation, or conduct an experiment. If the learning experiences are designed without sufficient information regarding the input state, they may not provide the appropriate "road map" to help the student progress from the starting point to the targeted end of the educational journey.

APPLYING THE MODEL

Having looked at an overview of our model, let us consider how the model can be applied in various educational settings and situations. We will do this in the context of a hypothetical undergraduate chemistry course. We will begin by applying the model to the process of course design and then continue to see how the model can serve as an important tool for the instructor whose job it is to help the learner to learn as each component of the course is implemented.

DESIGNING THE COURSE

Professor B is planning an introductory chemistry course for undergraduates. The course will include a "lecture" component, a lab component, and a "recitation" or lab discussion component. The course has published prerequisites that includes completion of high school chemistry and algebra courses.

To establish the output state objectives for the course, Professor B asks, "What should the students be able to do when they leave this course?" He decides that the students should be able to:

1. Use the symbolic language of chemistry to describe a chemical process;
2. Carry out simple chemical calculations to predict chemical states and the results of chemical reactions;
3. Develop and use models at the nano (particle) level to describe a variety of chemical phenomena;
4. Use chemical models to describe natural phenomena such as acid rain, global warming, and nuclear energy;
5. Extrapolate or extend chemistry concepts to more complex molecules such as organic molecules, polymers, and biomolecules; and
6. Apply chemistry concepts to new situations.

Professor B has established the criteria that define the output state or goal for the course. Note that each of the items on Professor B's list requires the student to *use* information, not merely memorize information.

If Professor B's job is helping the learner to learn, his next step must be to gain some information about the input state of his students. By establishing prerequisites for the course, Professor B has made some assumptions about the input state. He assumes that students will come to his class with a reasonable foundation in elementary chemistry and algebra. Furthermore, he has some expectation that most of the students who have completed the prerequisite courses will be able to apply the information that they learned to situations that were not specifically discussed in high school courses. Based on these expectations and, perhaps, some other information about the student population, such as their reading ability and facility with language, Professor B forms a mental image of the input state of his students.

With this in mind, Professor B designs a series of learning activities that he believes will help the students move from the input state to the output state. In the case of this specific course, he has prepared lectures, problem-solving exercises, discussion topics, and laboratory exercises that he believes will help students move from the input state to the output state. He has assembled pertinent materials into a syllabus for the course that will be distributed on the first day of class.   .

The success of these learning experiences depends, to a large extent, on the accuracy of Professor B's assumptions about the input state of his students. If, for example, he overestimates the capabilities of his students at the time they enter the course, they may not be prepared for the complexity of the educational experiences he has designed. If he underestimates the students' preparation, the students may find the educational experiences insufficiently challenging to maintain their interest in the course at a level that promotes their active engagement in the scheduled learning experiences.

How accurate are Professor B's assumptions? How well do faculty actually know the input state of students entering their courses? Rovick and his colleagues (Rovick et al., 1999) asked this question of a group of physiology faculty. The results of their study showed that even faculty with many years of teaching experience do not have an accurate understanding of the knowledge base and skills demonstrated by entering undergraduate students.

What are the implications of Rovick et al.'s study (1999) for Professor B's course design? Can Professor B design learning experiences if he does not know the specific input state of his entering students, or must he wait until he can assess the input state before designing learning experiences intended to help the students reach the desired output state? Of course he prepares a set of learning experiences for the course. But he must recognize that this set of activities represents a "box of tools" for learning. Some of the tools may prove to be appropriate for the knowledge and skills level of the incoming students, and some may turn out not to be appropriate. However, only after Professor B assesses the input state of his students can he determine how to best use the tools that he has designed. Some may be used as they were designed, some will have to be discarded, and some may require modification to provide students with the help that they need in moving from the input state to the desired output state.

How can Professor B assess the input state of the students in his course? He can, of course, administer a pre-test to students enrolled in his course at the beginning of the academic term. The results of this assessment can be used to guide his further planning for the course.

However, it is also important to recognize that the model we have described is not just for use in designing a course or curriculum. It is applicable to every learning activity that makes up the course. Thus, determining the input state of the students is not a one-time task, it is an on-going task. In a sequence of learning activities, the output state for one activity becomes the input state for the subsequent activity. With this in mind, our model representation can be modified as shown in Figure 3.2. With this modification, it is clear to see that assessing the output state for one activity is part of the assessment of the input state for the next activity.

It is clear from this representation that obtaining information about the input state is part of a continuing, iterative process. However, this is not as daunting as it seems at first glance. While it is not necessary to conduct a formal assessment at each step of the way, it is necessary that the instructor interact with the students in some way that will provide information about what the students know, what they can do, and how they are thinking. The purpose of determining the input state is to give the instructor guidance in helping the learner to learn. Once the instructor has information concerning the input state, he or she can determine how to use the planned learning experience to best help the students reach the output state. Using our analogy of an educational journey, the input state helps the instructor determine which "route" on the educational roadmap is most likely to be the shortest path to the output state.

SUMMARY

We have presented a model that we use to think about all educational activities. The model, coupled with our belief that the instructor's job is to help the learner to learn, provides guidance in all situations in which we hope to foster meaningful learning. The process begins with establishing goals for the output state. The goals may be extensive for a course or curriculum, or they may be relatively simple for the answer to a specific question asked

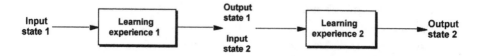

FIG. 3.2. The model as applied to sequential learning experiences.

within the context of a particular topic. The next step is to assess the input state. The output state defines our destination. The input state defines our starting point. The learning experiences that we provide the student represent the various paths that can be taken to help the student move from the input state to the output state. It is important to recognize that, if the output goal is to be able to complete a task, the learning experiences must contain opportunities to practice completing that task.

Defining the desired output state can be challenging. It requires that we be very explicit in our expectations for our students' learning. We will examine this process in more detail in the next chapter.

Assessing the input state is also critical to the process, and there are many ways of assessing the input state. The critical element of the assessment is that the instructor must interact with students in ways that reveal what students are thinking and how they use the information that they currently have. We will discuss various ways of assessing the input state in subsequent chapters.

Part II

Roles for the Teacher in Creating an Active Learning Environment

4

Defining the Output State

CHAPTER OVERVIEW

The output state is the goal that you set for any educational experience. It is what you expect the students to be able to do at the completion of that experience. What you define as your output state depends on many factors including the educational level of your students. If meaningful learning, or learning with understanding, is your goal, the description of your desired output state must include both what knowledge is to be accumulated and what the students are expected to be able to do with that knowledge.

In Chapter 3, we proposed a general model of the educational process. In this chapter, we examine in more detail the output state of that model. Our goal here is to illustrate the power of defining the output state as the first step in helping the learner to learn. We will do this by: (1) providing a clearer picture of what we mean by the output state, (2) examining how we go about defining the output state and some of the factors that must be considered in doing so, (3) discussing how our definitions of the output state are communicated to our students, (4) illustrating the power of defining the output state as the first step in the process of helping the learner to learn, and, (5) discussing how defining the output state contributes to more effective assessment.

Before proceeding, however, it is important to ask, "When do we pay attention to setting output state goals?" Do we only define an output state for the course as a whole? Obviously, the answer is "No!" Setting goals for the output state is appropriate for every learning experience in a course. Output state goals can be set for a 5-minute class discussion, a 2-hour problem-solving workshop, a laboratory session, a unit focused on a particular topic, or the entire course. If a student asks a question, for example, we must think about the output state of this exchange so that we can provide an appropriate answer or engage in a meaningful dialogue. The necessity for setting output goals is inherent in *everything* that we do in the classroom.

WHAT DO WE MEAN BY THE EXPECTED OUTPUT STATE?

The idea of setting explicit learning objectives or performance objectives is not new. Bloom's *Taxonomy of Educational Objectives* appeared in 1956, and learning objectives began appearing in textbooks in the late 1970s and early 1980s. The list in Table 4.1 is taken from a medical physiology text that was published in 1983 (Brown & Stubbs, 1983). This list appears before the first chapter which deals with membrane transport. Note that the objectives tell the student that, after reading the chapter, he should be able to account for things, describe things, discuss things, distinguish between things, and understand things. The authors do not expand on what they mean by "understand" or how students will know if they do "understand." Statements of learning objectives set by authors have not changed much in the intervening years. Table 4.2 contains a list of learning objectives from an introductory anatomy and physiology textbook published in 2000 (Seeley, Stephens, & Tate, 2000). Again, the objectives are for students to describe things, define things, compare things, contrast things, distinguish between things, and explain things. To achieve these objectives, students must acquire knowledge, but they do not necessarily have to integrate that knowledge into a coherent mental model that can be used to solve problems. Defining "understanding" is left up to the student, who is likely to think that she "understands" when she can repeat the description of the phenomenon that appears in the text or in her lecture notes.

TABLE 4.1
Learning objectives from a medical physiology textbook *circa* 1983

- Account for the selective barrier properties of the cell plasma membrane toward ions and molecules.
- Distinguish between equilibrium and steady states.
- Relate inward and outward fluxes across the plasma membrane.
- Describe the factors relating osmotic pressure to solute concentration.
- Discuss the factors involved in ultrafiltration.
- Understand how mediated transport differs from simple diffusion.

Note: From Brown & Stubbs (1983).

TABLE 4.2

Learning objectives from beginning anatomy and physiology text *circa* 2000

- Describe the structure of the plasma membrane. Explain why the plasma membrane is more permeable to lipid-soluble substances and small molecules than to large water-soluble substances.
- Describe the structure and function of the nucleus and nucleoli.
- Define cytoplasm, cytosol, and organelle.
- Contrast microtubules, microfilaments, and intermediate filaments.
- Compare the structure and function of rough and smooth endoplasmic reticulum.
- Explain the role in secretion of the Golgi apparatus and secretory vesicles.
- Distinguish between lysosomes and peroxisomes.

Note: From Seeley, Stephens, & Tate (2000).

But, if our goal is meaningful learning, and if we are to help the learner to learn, we must help students build mental models that can be used to solve problems or predict the behavior of the system being studied.

BEFORE PROCEEDING!

Look at the first objective in Tables 4.1 and 4.2. How would you modify them to obtain an output state objective that promotes meaningful learning?

So, the output state objective should reflect how the student is expected to use information. One possibility for an output state objective related to the structure and function of the cell membrane is to predict how a molecule with certain characteristics will be transported across the cell membrane and explain the basis for the prediction. Certainly, the relevant learning objectives listed in Tables 4.1 and 4.2 represent part of the route that the students must traverse to reach the output state objective, but they are only preliminary steps to achieving the objective of meaningful learning.

Recall from Chapter 3 that Professor B's first output state objective for his introductory chemistry course was for students to be able to use the symbolic language of chemistry to describe a chemical process. In learning how to use the symbolic language of chemistry, the student must certainly memorize and be able to recite certain terms making up the language of chemistry. However, memorization and recitation are not output state goals themselves. They are steps along the way to that goal. Having learned the "syntax" of the language, Professor B expects the student to be able to use that language to discuss, demonstrate, and explain what will happen in one or more chemical processes.

The output state objective, then, should describe what the student *should be able to do* upon completing the learning experience rather than merely describing the knowledge that should be acquired. The output state objective must be focused on a topic of manageable size, and it must be explicit. It is not sufficient, for example, for the objective to state that the student should be able to solve a problem. The type of problem to be solved must be stated. For example, the student should be able to: calculate pKa of the chemical reaction, or predict the trajectory of a falling object, or explain the decrease in the deer population when a new predator is introduced. The targeted skills must be evident from the statement of the objective.

DEFINING THE EXPECTED OUTPUT STATE: HOW TO DO IT AND WHAT TO THINK ABOUT

Defining output state objectives may not be as easy a task as defining "traditional" learning objectives. Because the output state objectives we have been discussing are process-oriented rather than content-oriented, it is necessary to think carefully and deeply about the processes involved when defining the objectives. For example, a number of different skills and a great deal of knowledge is necessary for students to correctly predict the responses of the cardiovascular system to changes in blood pressure, and these requirements are not obvious on inspection of the problem (Michael & Rovick, personal communication).

The objectives must be appropriate for the students' "level" of study. For example, the expectations related to a certain topic in an introductory course are not the same as the objectives dealing with the same topic in an intermediate or advanced-level course. For example, the degree of difficulty of the problems to be solved (predicting the results of a particular disturbance in the system) will be less in an introductory course than in an advanced course.

Defining appropriate output state objectives requires reflection on the part of the instructor. Rather than just deciding that the student should know this or that content, the instructor must decide how this or that content contributes to the goal defined by the output state objective. This process may seem very time-consuming. However, with practice, it becomes second nature. Certainly, focusing on helping the learner to learn helps in this development, for you can't help the learner progress if you don't have a destination in mind.

This process of reflection helps the instructor recognize the essential steps that the student must take to reach the targeted output state. The next question, after having established an output state objective, is to ask what the student needs to know and needs to be able to do to achieve the target objective. A series of these questions helps define the learning experiences and the sequence of learning experiences that are necessary to help the learner reach the output goals. Furthermore, as we shall see in subsequent chapters, the targeted output state provides an anchor for the process of helping the student move from the input state to the output state. When students begin to wander from the path that the instructor has chosen to move from the input to output states, or when it is apparent that an alternate path is more appropriate for a group of students, the output state objectives serve as a beacon to which the learning path can be directed.

HOW DO YOUR STUDENTS KNOW WHAT YOU EXPECT?

Having defined for yourself what you expect your students to be able to do when they complete a particular learning experience, or the entire course, it is essential that your goals be communicated to your students. Learning should never be a game of "guess what the teacher wants me to be able to do."

The obvious starting point is to "publish" your expectations in sufficient detail to enable your students to reach the goals you have established for your course. It will help if you also make available examples of what you mean by "compare and contrast," "explain," "predict," etc. In addition, it is important that you model these actions in your interactions with students and that you give students the opportunity to practice them. You can start by explicitly "comparing and contrasting" sedimentary and igneous rocks. You can then ask the students, working in small groups, to compare and contrast igneous and metamorphic rocks. Modeling the process and providing opportunities for practice will make your expectations clearer to your students than simply reading a description of what you think these mean.

THE RELATIONSHIP BETWEEN
THE OUTPUT STATE AND YOUR ASSESSMENT

Establishing a set of output state objectives that are based on what the student should be able to do at the end of the learning experience(s) should then direct the assessment process. If the expectation is that the student should be able *to do* something, your approach to assessment must determine if, indeed, she or he can do it. If the goal is to be able to make predictions and explain the basis for the prediction, assessment may consist of completing a prediction table with justification for some or all of the predictions. If the goal is to solve a certain kind of problem, the assessment instrument would be expected to include an appropriate problem to be solved.

Furthermore, if the instructor has been reflective in establishing the goals for the output state, and, as a result, the key steps in the process have been identified, a diagnostic element can be incorporated into the assessment. The issue is to determine how successful the student has been at reaching key intermediate steps. Questions may determine if appropriate knowledge was acquired. Assigned tasks may test to see if the student is able to complete one or more intermediate steps successfully. It is important to recognize that the assessment process must always be consistent with the targeted output goals. If, for example, the assessment consists solely of questions that require only recall of information, establishment of the output state objectives has been a futile process. It has been like running an experiment without gathering any data. We will return to the topic of assessment in subsequent chapters.

In this chapter, we have focused on the output state in our model. We have seen that setting output state objectives based on our expectations of what students should be able to do at the end of the learning experience(s) gives us a powerful tool in helping the learner to learn. It provides direction for designing appropriate learning experience(s); it serves as a beacon for the journey when the student seems to drift off course; and it guides the assessment process.

The output state objectives define where we want the students to go in their learning journey. If we are to help the learner to learn, we must assess, on a continuing basis, where the students are in their journey. Thus, our task in the next chapter is to examine the input state.

Chapter

5

Assessing the Input State:
The Teacher as Diagnostician

CHAPTER OVERVIEW

We need to know what our students know and what they can do in order to best determine how to help the learner to learn. That is to say, we must be diagnosticians in the classroom. The most direct way to find out what students know is to ask them. Continuous interaction with your students provides the information you need about their input state at the beginning of every learning experience. The various assessments that you do during the course can also serve to provide some of the needed information.

We have discussed setting objectives for the output state. These objectives reflect our expectations for what students should be able to do when they complete any learning experience. If our job is helping the learner to learn, the learning environment that we create will be a student-centered one in which the student is responsible for his or her own learning. To carry out our job, we must find out what kind of help the learner needs to achieve the output state goals that we have defined. In Chapter 3, we defined the input state as the knowledge and skills that the student brings to the educational component and the facility with which the student can use that knowledge and those skills. What do we really need to know about our students' input state and how do we get this information?

WHO ARE YOUR STUDENTS?

Students in the typical American classroom are an increasingly diverse group. They come from different socio-economic backgrounds and a variety of ethnic groups. Their cultural backgrounds can be quite different. For some, English is their mother tongue, but many others have learned English as a second or perhaps third language. Some learned English as young children, others learned it as an adult, and there are likely to be some students who are still in the process of becoming fluent in English. If we are committed to helping the learner to learn, it is essential that we understand something about the diversity present in our classroom.

Let's consider a situation in which it might matter a great deal. A colleague, born in Nigeria, spent many years in England as a graduate student and post-doctoral fellow. He eventually returned to Nigeria and found himself in the classroom. At some point he attempted to explain the concept of homeostasis and used a thermostatically controlled home heating system as an example. The blank looks on his students' faces finally caused him to pause, at which point he realized that none of his students had ever lived in a house with a furnace, let alone a thermostatically controlled one! Analogies only work when the learner has a relatively deep understanding of the original system.

Here is another example. Students for whom English is not their native language may have no problem reading the textbook or your syllabus, but they may find the wording of typical multiple choice questions very difficult to understand. A native Russian speaker asked the faculty proctor about the meaning of a particular question during the exam. When the proctor simply changed the order of the clauses in the stem of the question, the student immediately understood what was being asked in the question.

So, one important function of any attempt to interact with your students as a diagnostician is to understand the language or cultural differences that may impact their ability to understand what you expect them to master.

WHAT DO THEY KNOW COMING INTO YOUR COURSE?

Faculty readily accept the notion that prerequisite courses contribute to the input state of students entering their courses. The expectation is that if students have successfully completed the prerequisite courses, they know all of the content of those courses *and* they can utilize that knowledge and those skills in the context your course. The reality is that students *may* remember some of the content of the prerequisite courses, and they *may* be able to apply some of what they learned to the new course. However, they are just as likely *not* to remember specifics from the prerequisite course (McDermott, 1991), or they remember the content but cannot apply it in the context of your course.

Equally important, even experienced faculty may not have an accurate assessment of what their students know and can do as a result of the prerequisite courses (Rovick et al., 1999); there is a tendency to underestimate the students' factual knowledge and to overestimate their ability to apply that knowledge. So relying on knowledge of the courses that you have listed as prerequisites probably leaves you knowing less about the input state of your students than you need.

SOME OF WHAT STUDENTS KNOW IS NOT CORRECT

It is also important to recognize that some of what your students learned in previous courses was wrong. They may have misinterpreted something in the course, or, perhaps, they fully "understood" what they heard or read, but the way that the material was presented led to their building a faulty mental model.

In Chapter 1 we discussed learning as building mental models from existing and new information. Old knowledge is incorporated into, or related to, whatever is newly learned in one way or another. Every student, every learner, "knows" something about the topic to be learned. They may not realize this initially, and they may even deny it. However, they have acquired a vast storehouse of knowledge from personal experience in the physical world, from interactions with parents, siblings and friends, from the media, and from the very language that they use.

Some of the knowledge in this storehouse is "correct," but some is wrong in whole or in part. The "wrong" knowledge has been categorized by investigators and labeled by a growing number of terms intended to provide information about the cognitive aspects of these conceptual and reasoning difficulties (e.g., misconceptions, alternative conceptions, and naive theories; see Wandersee et al., 1994). The significance of the presence of this "wrong" knowledge is that it inevitably interferes with the learner's attempt to incorporate new, correct knowledge that is to be learned into that which is already known.

Regardless of their origins, expression of this "wrong" information by students can be considered diagnostic signs of problems with the process of conceptualization or problems with the reasoning process (Michael et al., 2002). In our terms, they are diagnostic of students' faulty mental models. If we are to help the learner to learn, we must probe our students to discover these diagnostic signs and attempt to identify the underlying problem with conceptualization or reasoning. In this way, we can bring the "problem" to the learners' attention and help the learner revise her or his mental model in a way that yields more accurate predictions of how the system being studied behaves.

THERE IS LIFE OUTSIDE OF YOUR CLASSROOM

There may also be other factors, factors that are not related to the students' knowledge base, that will impact student learning and thus represent aspects of the students' input state that we need to understand. For example, students may be single parents with the financial and social pressures that impact their learning. The students in your course are most likely taking a number of other courses simultaneously, each of them making demands on the students' time and effort. You need to know if and when these demands are affecting your students.

It should be evident from this discussion that assessing the input state is not a one-time task that occurs at the beginning of the course. It is a process that must continue throughout the duration of the course because the input state for course activities continues to change.

BEFORE PROCEEDING!

Reflect for a moment on how you currently assess the input state of your students. What will you do differently now that your approach to being a teacher is becoming focused on helping the learner to learn?

HOW DO YOU DIAGNOSE YOUR STUDENTS' INPUT STATE?

The key to assessing the input state on a regular basis is to interact with the learners. That is, we must engage the students in a dialogue. This is the only way that we can determine what they know and what they can do with the information that they possess and, hence, determine the kind of help the students need. To illustrate this, let's return to Professor B's chemistry course that we encountered in Chapter 3 and consider various ways that Professor B interacts with his students to gain information about their input state.

In the lecture hall, Professor B is about to embark on a new topic. Instead of launching into a lecture, he begins by asking the students to "Tell me what you know about this." He follows this by a series of probing questions to gain some insight about the depth of the knowledge that they exhibit. This exercise need not take much time, and it provides valuable information to help him implement the planned learning experiences in a productive way. He may now proceed with his lecture as originally planned; he may choose to spend less time discussing one topic that the students seem familiar with in favor of another topic with which they are less familiar; or he may decide that the class requires some help with prerequisite knowledge before he delivers his prepared lecture. By knowing what is review and what is new, Professor B is in a better position to address the needs of the students during this class period.

In a variant of this approach, Professor B has the class work in small groups for several minutes to see what important elements of the forthcoming topic might already be familiar to them. For example, before discussing the properties of gases, he asks students to draw a graph of the effect of pressure changes on the volume of a gas. He then asks the groups to describe their graph. He may do this in a number of ways. He may call on a group to report their results, or he may have the groups exchange papers and have one group describe another group's graph.

Having the groups report their answers provides him with information about the input state. However, this approach promotes another important element of learning. This exercise helps students explicitly state their expectations for the key elements of the discussion. In doing so, *they* examine their current knowledge state (input state) for links to the learning experience in which they are about to engage. In this way, they are better prepared to identify aspects of the learning experience that are review, identify aspects that are new, and recognize how what they already know is connected to the new material.

In yet another situation, Professor B acquires information about the input state using a slightly different approach. In this case, he presents the class with a problem or experiment and asks the students to make a prediction based on their knowledge of the system being discussed. The prediction is qualitative in nature (e.g., something will increase, decrease, or exhibit no change), and the class can be polled by a show of hands to see what their predictions are. It is important in this scenario to provide an "I don't know" or similar option, as, at this point in the course, this may be an honest response. Professor B can ask individual students for their answers, or he can provide several minutes for the students to discuss the issue with their neighbors before making a prediction. Professor B can choose to focus on the "correct" answer, or he may ask students who have predicted "incorrectly" what the rationale was for their prediction. This provides another non-threatening way to learn more about the input state. The students have committed to a position, and all that Professor B is doing is gathering more information about the thought process that contributed to that answer.

This information, especially if a large portion of the class makes errors in their predictions, informs Professor B about pathways for helping the learner to learn. Again, having this insight, he may choose to use scheduled learning experiences as he originally planned; he may modify them to emphasize certain aspects or de-emphasize others; or he may choose to postpone the scheduled learning experiences in favor of laying a better foundation for helping his students achieve the output state.

On another occasion, Professor B uses a figure as a visual aid in his lecture, and he wants to know the input state with respect to his students' understanding of the relationships shown in the figure. To gain this information, Professor B asks the students to tell him what they see in the figure. If their descriptions indicate that the students have extracted the appropriate information from the figure, he can reemphasize the important points and move on. However, if the answers that the students provide indicate confusion about the mechanism that was depicted, he can address this confusion so that the students have a better chance of reaching the desired output state for this activity.

It is important to recognize that the way such "diagnostic" questions are asked is important. If Professor B expects students to participate in the process, he must make the learning environment a safe one in which students feel comfortable taking the risk of answering the questions. One way to do this with a figure or other type of pictorial is to ask the student, "What do you see?" This question can be asked in any classroom environment. There is no risk in answering the question as there is no right or wrong answer; whatever the student sees, she sees. The instructor can then ask, "Who else sees this same thing?" This question will lead to affirmation of what the initial student saw, or it may lead to other interpretations of the message of the figure. In either case, the instructor learns something about the input state of the students, and this information provides direction for choosing the path that will best lead these students to the output state. In addition, the students begin to realize that different people may have different interpretations of the same visual information, and that it is important to seek clarification if everyone is to obtain the same information from the pictorial.

The examples that we have considered were all situated in the lecture hall. However, it is not difficult to see that these techniques are equally valid for assessing the input state in the other components (discussion section, laboratory) of Professor B's course.

The take-home message from each of these examples is that assessing the input state provides direction for the learning experience required to reach the target output state goals. Furthermore, engaging in these types of dialogue at the end of the activity provides an indication of how successful we have been in helping students reach the desired output state. This output state is, of course, the input state for the next step in the progression of the course.

THE IMPORTANCE OF STUDENT LANGUAGE

For the instructor who has adopted the "helping the learner to learn" mindset, each class period is a diagnostic exercise aimed at gaining a better understanding of the problems that students have in building appropriate mental models of the systems being discussed. In many cases these "problems" are related to the ways in which the students use, or understand, the language of the discipline.

What steps does this instructor take to determine if, and where, students are having problems building appropriate mental models? The instructor interacts with the students. We have discussed some of Professor B's approaches to this interaction, and we have seen how the responses serve as diagnostic clues. We will discuss other classroom techniques that provide diagnostic information in Chapters 8 to 11.

There is much to be learned about a student's mental model by listening to the language that he or she uses. Consider, for example, the concept of homeostasis, one of the central organizing concepts in physiology. A textbook definition of homeostasis is the ability of the body to maintain a relatively constant internal environment (Silverthorn, 2001). Students often interpret this to mean that, when perturbed, the body will return the internal environment to "normal." When confronted with a pathophysiological situation, a student may explain that "the body wants to (or needs to) return to normal, so compensatory changes will occur, and, eventually, the system will return to normal."

This apparently simple statement raises several critical questions in the mind of the diagnostician with respect to the student's mental model. First, does the student believe that, given enough time, the regulatory systems of the body can "overcome" any malfunction of the system? Does the student recognize that "compensatory changes" can only occur within the scope of the existing regulatory mechanisms and that the body cannot utilize "compensatory mechanisms" that are not inherent to the body's systems? Does the student recognize that a stable internal environment does not necessarily mean that all parameters of that environment are at "normal" values?

Another related example is the student who, when confronted with the description of a patient whose arterial carbon dioxide levels were high because of chronic lung disease, exclaimed, "He needs to reduce his arterial P_{CO_2}!" The implication of her statement, which was confirmed by follow-up questioning, was that this individual could not possibly live with his high arterial P_{CO_2} levels, and that, unless the body figured out some way to reduce these levels, death was imminent. Her mental model of homeostasis was flawed. She did not recognize that, in this patient, the mechanisms that would normally return arterial P_{CO_2} to a normal level were compromised. Consequently, the system could not operate at a normal level, but homeostasis was established at a new level where carbon dioxide levels were elevated.

The language that a student uses when asking a question may often lead to confusion for other class members. The problem may be related to the student's imprecise use of language, or the student's language may reflect a faulty mental model. In either case, it is important to the student asking the question and to the students listening to the question and response that the instructor's response address the issue in a way that will clarify the issue for all students in the class

Our approach to such questions is to restate the question as defined by the words that the student used and then restate it based on our interpretation of the student's mental model. Hence two questions are answered. The first is prefaced by the words, "This is the question that I heard you ask." The interpretation of the words that the student used is then presented followed by an answer. The second response is prefaced by the words, "This is the question that I think you were trying to ask." This question is then stated, and the answer is provided or prompted from other students. By carrying out this type of dialogue, students begin to recognize the importance of language, and they begin to think critically about the mental models that they are building. They, too, become diagnosticians and facilitators of learning because they begin to listen to their colleagues' questions and explanations in a more analytical way, and they enter into the discussion, helping to provide new insights for their colleagues.

It should be obvious at this point that it is essential that the diagnostician practice the skill of "listening" if such interactions are to be successful. Too often, we tend to fall into the same trap as our students. Instead of *listening* to everything that a student asks or says, we pick key words from the question or statement and, based on what the key words mean to us, provide a response. As a result, we often do not answer the student's question, and worse, we discourage the student from asking more questions or contributing to the class discussion. "If this instructor doesn't listen to my question, why should I bother to ask?"

THE ROLE OF COURSE ASSESSMENTS
IN DIAGNOSING THE INPUT STATE

In most courses a variety of assessment tools are used to determine the grade that the student has earned. We will discuss assessment in Chapter 12. Here is it important to point out that formal course assessments, whether assigned papers, lab reports, oral presentations or quizzes and exams, also can provide information about the input state of the students. It is important to ask not only if the student response is "right" or "wrong" but to determine how the students are thinking about a particular phenomenon. In this way the results of some assessment exercise can tell you about the mental models that the students have built.

For example, a group of students in a physiology course answered an exam question about the body's responses to an acidosis. Although their scores on this question were generally satisfactory, a closer examination of their answers revealed a widespread error in their mental model describing the determinants of ventilation (Michael, 1998). As a consequence the instructor was able to use the next available opportunity in the classroom to encourage the students to test their mental model further and in this way begin the process of repairing it.

SUMMARY

By adopting the helping the learner to learn mindset, we become diagnosticians in the classroom, entering into a dialogue with a single student, a small group of students, or the whole class and *listening* to the students' responses. The goal is to assess the input state. By analyzing the apparent meaning of the responses that students provide, we attempt to gain insight into the state of their current mental models and where they may be having problems in the conceptualization or reasoning processes. By responding in an appropriate way, we can help the students recognize where their errors arise and help them to revise their mental models. Through this process, a range of "problems" can be diagnosed, and remediation of the problems can be facilitated. Facilitating movement from the input state to the targeted output goals leads us to the learning activities that we design to help the learner make this transition. We examine issues related to the development of these activities in the next chapter.

Chapter

6

Moving From the Input to the Output State: The Learning Experience

CHAPTER OVERVIEW

If we are to help the learner to learn, we must provide our students with learning experiences that will move them from their input state to our expected output state. These experiences can occur in the lecture hall, conference room, or student laboratory. Wherever they occur, the key feature of a successful learning experience is that it facilitate the students' testing of their mental models. Accomplishing this does not mean discarding everything you have done before or creating totally new learning resources. It means that you must use your resources in a different way.

Our job is to help the learner to learn. In Chapter 4 we defined the output state as a set of goals describing what the student should be able to do with the mental model(s) that he or she is building during a particular educational component. This is the destination for our educational journey. In Chapter 5 we discussed the need to assess the input state (the point of origin for the journey) so that we have an idea of the kind of help that the learner needs to reach the targeted output state. We can now focus on what lies between the input and the output states by addressing the question, "what kinds of learning experiences can we offer students to help them move from the input to the output state?"

When examining this question, we must keep in mind that responsibility for learning lies with the learner. We cannot learn for the learner. This means that the learner must actively engage in the process of building and testing his or her mental models. In other words, the learning experiences that we provide our students must contribute to creating an active learning environment for them.

53

What kinds of learning experiences can we provide students to help them move from the input to the output state? The initial response to this question is that there are a wealth of activities depending on the classroom environment on which we choose to focus. In the laboratory, we can provide a variety of experiments and demonstrations. In small group sessions, we can provide problems to be solved. If we focus on large group settings, here too we can provide problems to solve or experiments to run. The range of activities we can offer spans the spectrum from a carefully formulated answer to a student's question, to presenting a graph or a figure to be analyzed, to posing a problem to be solved, to having students run an experiment either in the classroom or the laboratory, to giving information to students either in a hand-out or as a "mini-lecture." The activity may involve individual students, groups of two or three students, or larger groups of students. We will present specific examples of using these activities when we discuss the physical environments of the lecture hall, conference room, and student laboratory in the ensuing chapters.

A more fundamental answer to the question, however, is that we need to provide learning experiences that help students build and test their mental models. Such an experience can be as simple as asking a student in the classroom or laboratory who has made an erroneous prediction what the consequences of that prediction might be. "If your prediction is correct, what will happen next? Is that what actually happens?" It may be how we interact with a student or a group of students. For example, rather than describing a graph to a group of students in a laboratory discussion session, we might ask, "what does this graph tell you about the relationship between the variables?" The learning experience may be more complex. For example, in a chemistry setting, the task may be to work with a computer-simulated reaction or explain the basis for an animation of a reaction. It may be to work together to solve a case problem in an ecology class. In each of these examples, the student must address his or her mental model and test its appropriateness to the situation at hand.

HOW DO I PREPARE RESOURCES
FOR THE LEARNING EXPERIENCE?

At first glance, the process that we have outlined seems to suggest that the successful instructor must be a psychic, anticipating every possible problem that students may have and preparing suitable learning experiences to address each of these problems. In fact, a common reaction among faculty introduced to the helping the learner to learn mindset is that adopting it would necessitate discarding the classroom materials that they have developed or collected, abandoning the teaching strategies and tactics that have "worked" for them in the past, and, in one sense, starting their teaching careers anew. To them, this change in point of view represents an insurmountable challenge, for instead of merely refining lecture outlines, laboratory exercises, and visual aids for a particular class, they must be prepared to address the needs of a variety of students. In addition, they must develop appropriate activities, along with supporting resource material, to meet all of these potential needs. Preparing for class must also include anticipating the unknown, an impossible task, and having solutions at hand for unknown problems.

Fortunately, adopting the helping the learner to learn mindset does *not* mean discarding the past and starting over. The process of preparing resource material for class is essentially the same. What is different is the way that these aids and resources are used in the classroom. They are used in a way that helps students test the mental models that they are building. Thus, the questions that must be kept in mind are, "What problems do I anticipate my students will have when working with the pertinent information?" and "What resources do I need to help the students recognize the problems they are having?" Sometimes the resources we have in hand need some modification. For example, in the student laboratory, a lab protocol may need to be rewritten in a way that encourages students to make predictions about the outcomes of their experiments, compare the outcomes with their predictions, and reconcile the differences between their expectations and their observations (see chap. 10). However, in other instances, the resource material at hand may serve the purpose of helping the learner to learn very well.

Consider, for example, Professor W, who uses case studies in his teaching. In the past, he handed out the entire case description including the lab results. The students would then attempt to solve the case with all of the information regarding the case at hand. Since adopting the helping the learner to learn mindset, he uses the same cases in a slightly different way. He now presents the case description one step at a time. In this way, he simulates the process that the students would follow if they were confronted with this case in "real life." At each step, he prompts the students to discuss how they interpret the information at hand and what they expect to find at the next step. For example, the students are now asked to suggest what *they* think might be appropriate laboratory tests to run and how they might interpret the results of those tests. The class then moves on to consider the next piece of information that is available.

What has changed here? In the first application, the learning experience did not force the students to move through the problem-solving process in a way that forced them to think about, and articulate, their mental models. In the current situation, the students are continually confronting and testing their mental models that relate to the case study. In this instance, Professor W's materials preparation simply required him to reformat the case description. Furthermore, Professor W could use this exercise in a "lecture" environment or in a small group discussion session.

AS THE INSTRUCTOR, WHAT MUST I DO TO IMPLEMENT SUCCESSFUL LEARNING EXPERIENCES?

Successful implementation of learning experiences often depends on the nature of interaction between the instructor and the students. By carrying on a dialogue with the learners, the instructor can discover which route best matches the experience and views of the *learners*. The "lecture," for example, becomes a discussion in which the instructor continually obtains feedback to assess whether the learners are having difficulty over some part of the terrain or, perhaps, even getting lost along the way. A figure that had been used as an expository tool ("this figure shows that ... ") becomes an inquiry tool with which students can test and discuss their mental models ("what does this figure tell you?"). In the student laboratory, well-placed questions in a dialogue carried out with the students as they conduct the experiment lead students to test their mental models ("what do you think you will see in this part of the experiment?"). By interacting with students, the instructor often discovers that what he or she anticipated as "problem" areas do not necessarily lead to confusion. However, what he or she thought were "simple" steps (e.g., word definitions, "logical" conclusions) may cause considerable confusion. By engaging in an interactive process, the teacher can guide the students along the most appropriate path to the day's destination. Remember, the instructor's output objectives serve as the destination for the day's journey. If he or she is familiar with the terrain, it shouldn't make any difference to him or her which particular path is used to reach to the destination. If the objectives are met, the student will have constructed and will be able to use a mental model consistent with the defined objectives.

The helping the learner to learn mindset also helps the instructor focus more on the process of learning which, in turn, can help students engage in activities that make them more aware of the challenges of building appropriate mental models. To illustrate this, consider the following scenario. Professor M has given an exam in which students are required to justify their answer to some multiple choice questions. A significant number of students choose incorrect answers to one question, and their explanations reveal several errors that the students have when thinking about the aspect of the system that is the focus of the question. To help students examine their mental models, Professor M brings a sampling of the explanations to the class and, in small group discussions, has them discuss the types of mental model errors that might lead to these explanations. This exercise helps students with faulty mental models recognize where their difficulties lie, and it helps students with appropriate mental models reinforce those models.

HOW DO I PREPARE TO IMPLEMENT
THE LEARNING EXPERIENCES?

Colleagues who visit our classrooms and attendees of our workshops often comment that they can't do in their classrooms what we do in our classrooms. When asked to elaborate on what they mean, they describe a perceived spontaneity and creativity in the way we move the class in a certain direction by asking questions and eliciting answers. In their view, our preparation for class must include developing a database of responses and examples that would fit any conceivable classroom situation.

In reality, our preparation is not substantially different from theirs. What is different, however, is our mindset in the classroom. We are in the classroom to help the learner to learn. Our role is the same whether we are in the "lecture" hall, the small group workshop, the student laboratory, or working one-on-one with a student in our office. Through dialogue, we discover that the learner has a problem building an appropriate mental model. To fulfill our role, we must diagnose the problem and help the learner to overcome it. The problem might be due to nothing more than a lapse in attention, or it may be due to a fundamental misunderstanding of some aspect of the system being discussed or, in the case of a laboratory exercise, being investigated. The "spontaneity and creativity" seen by the casual observer is really a response to the student. We ask ourselves, "Why is this student having trouble?" After making a diagnosis, we ask, "How can I help this student solve the problem?" The response may be to repeat a question; it may be to help the student recognize the consequences of her mental model; or it may be to get some students to act out the steps of a mechanism.

It is important, then, to recognize that the instructor need not and, in fact, cannot anticipate every possible path to the targeted output state. But, the instructor does know where the destination lies. When necessary, he or she can redirect the students from the group's current position toward the journey's end. This direction is the key to providing successful learning experiences.

The ease with which the process can be adopted and its power in the classroom recently became apparent to one of the attendees of a workshop we were presenting. The assignment was to prepare a 10-minute mini-lesson that could be conducted either in a lecture or small group discussion setting. The mini-lesson could be focused on any topic. "Students" worked in groups of four, and each group was to set target output state goals, propose a means of assessing the input state, and propose learning activities to take the "class" from the input state to the targeted output state. One person from each group was to be the instructor for their mini-lesson and subsequently conduct the mini-lesson. The "class" consisted of undergraduate biology and life science teachers.

The instructor began her mini-lesson by asking the class a question related to the action of G-proteins. After a long silence, one person in the class answered the question. The instructor then asked another question directed at a more fundamental knowledge about G-proteins. After another pause, the same person answered the second question. The process was repeated a third time with the same results. It became apparent that the pauses were not a sign of reluctance on the part of members of the class to respond, but that only one person in the class had substantial prior knowledge of the major features of G-protein interactions.

The instructor then proceeded with her mini-lesson in what seemed to be a seamless interaction, and she reached her target "destination" in the remainder of the 10-minute period.

During the "reflection-discussion" period that followed her mini-lesson, the instructor remarked on how her assumptions regarding the class' input state had been wrong. Furthermore, without the explicit output state goals that her group had agreed upon, her mini-lesson would have been undermined because what she had planned to do did not meet the students' needs. Having her "destination" in mind, she was able to modify the learning experience "on the fly" and proceed in a meaningful way through the mini-lesson. She was surprised that the process seemed so natural for her.

"FRINGE BENEFITS" OF ADOPTING THE HELPING THE LEARNER TO LEARN MINDSET

Adopting the helping the learner to learn mindset can make a dramatic impact on the learning environment. Including assessment of the input state as an integral part of the learning environment and choosing appropriate learning activities to help the learner move toward the targeted output state provides opportunities for us, the instructors, to learn. Whatever their origin, the "problems" identified through dialogue with students present new challenges for us. These challenges make the classroom environment an active learning environment for us as well as the students. Furthermore, in this environment, students begin to focus on how they learn, instructors learn more about how their students do or don't learn their discipline, and both students and instructors can work together to maximize learning in the environment. Both students and instructor have an opportunity to test their mental models and gain new insights. Both students and instructors become facilitators of learning.

This outcome is predicated on the assumption that the students will, in fact, become willing participants in the learning environment. As anyone who is acquainted with the behavior of undergraduate students in the United States can tell you, most students are willing to sit in class and listen to what you have to tell them, but most are reluctant to participate in any meaningful way. If our model is to succeed, we must meet the challenge of getting our students to "buy into the game" and participate in the active learning environment. The next chapter addresses this challenge.

Part III

Creating Active Learning Environments

7

Preparing Students to Participate in an Active Learning Environment

CHAPTER OVERVIEW

The active learning environment will not flourish if students do not accept responsibility for their own learning and participate in the learning environment in an appropriate way. This chapter discusses issues related to getting students to recognize the need to take responsibility for their own learning and to recognize the need to engage in discussion with others in the learning environment. The chapter also discusses the need for creating a safe environment if student participation is to be expected, and ways in which the instructor can promote a safe learning environment. The instructor must also clearly and understandably define "the rules of the game" for the learner.

Our job is to help the learner to learn. It is the students' job to learn. We have discussed meaningful learning and what the learner must do to learn with understanding. The learner must actively engage in testing and refining the mental models that she or he is building. However, there is a crucial element needed for success that our model cannot guarantee. Students must be willing to participate in this process. In many cases, getting students to participate in classroom activities can be quite a challenge. So, the question is, "How do I get my students to 'play the game'?"

BEFORE PROCEEDING!

What, if anything, do you do at the beginning of your course to get your students to "play the game?" Do these things "work" to your satisfaction?

AN APPROACH TO THE PROBLEM

We can use our input state-learning experience-output state model (chap. 3) to productively think about approaches to this challenge. In this context, the desired output state is a learning environment in which students are actively engaged in building, testing, and refining mental models. This means that they ask questions when classroom presentations or discussions do not make sense to them. It also means that they are willing to reveal publicly what they are thinking and how they arrived at their conclusions. Finally, it means that they are willing to challenge their peers, either in small groups or within the context of a whole class discussion, to explore and explain their thinking process.

To some students this desired output state will be threatening and frightening, while other students will find it exhilarating and exciting. The difference depends, to a large extent, on the attitude that each student brings to the classroom. As we have defined the desired output state, students must be willing to take risks. They must be willing to admit vulnerability, display ignorance, and be intellectually argumentative. So, in preparing students to participate in this environment, we must convince students that the environment is safe, that accepting the risks will help them learn, and that the rewards of participation are worth the effort. If we are successful, our students will form a motivated learning community in which all community members are engaged in the process and for whom learning is fun.

THE INPUT STATE

Before we can decide how to reach the output state, we must consider the input state. Who are our students? What are their past experiences? How do their cultural backgrounds differ? What are their expectations about teaching and learning?

First we must remember that our student population is made up of individuals. Although all students may share **some** common experiences, they each have their own personal experiences that serve as the basis for their expectations and determine how they interpret what they hear and see.

One experience shared by most students is the passive learning environment that characterizes much of current schooling. In these learning environments, they were required to demonstrate only that they assimilated information that was disseminated in class. As a result, they became adept at organizing information in formats that are conducive to memorization but are not necessarily appropriate for building the integrated conceptual models necessary for analyzing scientific problems. In other words, they were not required to engage in meaningful learning. The academic reward system to which most students have become accustomed reflects this. Students perceive the reward system as being based on examination scores, not necessarily on meaningful learning. Hence, students want to know "the bottom line" rather than being concerned about the conceptual basis for the bottom line. Your job, in their view, is to tell them the correct answers, and, having the correct answers, they will know what they need to know to score well on exams and progress along their academic path.

Student expectations based on such shared experiences can lead to significant challenges that must be met when creating a successful active learning environment. However, instructors must also recognize that challenges based on diversity in the class (i.e., the students' individual experiences) also exist. Furthermore, to create a successful active learning environment, instructors must help students recognize that the inherent diversity in the class creates challenges for their learning. Instructors and students alike must understand that our interpretation of what we see and hear depends on our individual past experiences. Two people looking at the same picture do not necessarily glean the same meaning from it.

Our use of language also depends on our past experience. Although it is easy to recognize that interpretation of language (e.g., English) may constitute a source of confusion for students who have recently learned English, it is equally true that cultural differences or regional geographic differences in the use of language are often a source of confusion and miscommunication. Furthermore, age may constitute a source of miscommunication because common vocabulary and use of language are constantly changing. A colleague recently gave an examination in which the words, "taut" and "aperture," were used in two of the questions. He was appalled to learn that his students did not know the meaning of either word. After all, the words had been a part of his vocabulary for as long as he could remember.

THE LEARNING EXPERIENCE(S)

Given our assessment of the input state, what steps must we take to reach the output state of having students participate in our learning environment? It is clear that the learning experiences (classroom activities) that we design must focus on three goals. We must make sure that the students' expectations for the course match our expectations; we must help students recognize that they need to ask questions when clarification is needed; and we must convince the students that our learning environment is a safe one for them to engage in dialogue. Let us look at each of these goals and the ways in which they can be approached.

MATCHING EXPECTATIONS ABOUT TEACHING AND LEARNING

As already noted, many students arrive at our classrooms with considerable experience in passive learning environments. Because of this, their expectations about your course may or may not match your expectations about the course. Students may expect that you will tell them all they need to know to pass the exam. Hence, they may not regard it as necessary to interrupt the information flow to ask questions if something does not make sense. The time to ask questions is after class or during office hours. Even in laboratories, past experience has led students to believe that they will be told what to do, what to observe, and how to interpret those observations. Most students do not expect laboratory exercises to be inquiry driven.

If you expect students to engage in active learning, students must be made aware of the fact that they are expected to participate, that your job is not to tell them all they need to know, that they are responsible for their learning, and that your job is to help them to learn. If this is not done, you and your students are working at cross purposes, and there is little hope that meaningful learning will occur in the classroom.

How can you help students understand the expectations that form the basis for your course design and help them reorient their expectations to match your expectations? One approach is to merely extend the introductory comments given at the beginning of the course to include a description of the respective roles of instructor and student. Certainly, when students are told that you view your role in the classroom as a facilitator and, consequently, class time will be devoted to discussions in which students are expected to participate rather than lectures in which students are expected only to listen and take notes, students will understand what is expected of them.

However, with this approach, the instructor addresses expectations that he or she considers relevant. There may be student expectations that are relevant, but which have not been considered by the instructor. Furthermore, this approach fails to take advantage of an early opportunity to engage the class in the type of student-centered dialogue that is necessary if the instructor is to successfully help the learner to learn.

The following approach for aligning student and instructor expectations has been effective in our classrooms. Based on classroom assessment techniques described by Angelo and Cross (1993), the activity engages each student in a form of dialogue and demonstrates the instructor's desire to interact with the students. In addition, it provides an opportunity for the instructor to gain insight into the students' expectations so that these can be addressed specifically.

On the first day of class, blank 3 × 5-inch note cards are distributed to the class. The students are asked to write answers to the following two questions without putting their names on the cards. "What is my (the student's) job in this course?" and "What is your (the instructor's) job in this course?" The responses are then collected, and the instructor reads a sample of them to the class, discussing each with respect to his or her own expectations. In this way, the instructor's expectations for the course become known, but they are discussed in the context of the students' expectations.

This approach has several advantages in terms of getting students to "play the game." It immediately introduces the students to an interactive environment, and it lets the students know that you welcome and value student input. This message is critical if you expect students to participate in discussions. It also helps you gain some insight into the concerns of the students. This is valuable if your intent is to help the learner to learn.

To further illustrate what can be accomplished with this approach, let us consider several potential responses given by students and how you might address those responses. In response to the question regarding the student's job, a student writes that her job is to be prepared for class/lab. In some students' opinions, this might be stating the obvious, but the response offers you an opportunity to discuss what, in your opinion, it means to be prepared for this class or lab. Because the discussion is initiated by a student's comment, the class dynamic is different than it would be if you had simply provided this information as part of an introductory lecture.

Another student expects you to come to class with a well-thought-out, informative lecture that stresses the things that are important. In addition, she expects you to be available for questions. This provides an opportunity for you to tell the class that you do not intend to lecture, in a traditional sense, but rather that you intend to lead a discussion of the topic of the day. Furthermore, you not only expect students to ask questions after class and during office hours, but you also expect students to ask questions as part of the discussion.

A third student says that the instructor's job is to teach in a way that I (the student) can understand and that makes the subject come alive. Here the student has generated an opportunity for you to discuss what it means, in the context of your course, to "understand" something. In our courses, for example, "understanding" is demonstrated when the student can make correct predictions about the behavior of a system and is able to explain what will happen when that system is perturbed. This student's response also provides an opportunity for you to help the student gain insight into how the subject "came alive" for you. The issue of making the subject "come alive" raises the issue of student motivation. Here, again, is an opportunity to discuss how participating in your learning environment will lead to student meaningful learning, that the process can be fun, and that students will recognize that learning is occurring, thus strengthening motivation.

It is not necessary, in this exercise, to respond to each student's card at this time, since many of them express the same general theme. However, it is important for the instructor to read each card after class and respond at the beginning of the next class session to any relevant issues raised by student expectations that were not discussed in the previous class meeting. Addressing additional points raised by other students' cards the next day also emphasizes the message that their input is valued.

A word of caution is in order. Through this exercise, the instructor establishes the "rules of the game." He or she enters into a contract with the students. If the instructor expects students to "play" by these rules (i.e., comply with the contract), he or she must conduct the course in a manner consistent with those rules (i.e., he or she must also comply with the contract). For example, if the instructor tells the class that the goal of the course is to develop problem-solving skills, the course activities must include opportunities to engage in and practice problem solving. Furthermore, exams must test problem-solving skills rather than only recall of facts. If class activities and assessment are not consistent with the terms of the contract, the instructor breaks the contract and can no longer expect the students to comply with it.

HELPING STUDENTS RECOGNIZE
THE NEED TO SEEK CLARIFICATION

In order to appreciate the need to seek clarification, students must recognize that they may not interpret the meaning of words that they hear in the same way as their colleagues. Recognition of this fact is critical because communicating with our colleagues is one way that we test our mental models. Thus, effective communication is essential if students and instructor are to reach a common understanding of the phenomena being discussed. Students must recognize their need for clarification, and faculty must be willing to seek clarification from students so that the meaning of questions and comments may be clear to the whole class.

Most students will acknowledge the fact that two people can look at the same picture or hear the same words and interpret them in different ways. However, the potential impact of this fact on each student's own learning doesn't become evident until the students experience the problem firsthand and recognize how easily they can misinterpret or misunderstand what they see or hear. The challenge is to help students realize that differences in interpretation are a common occurrence.

There are many ways of helping students recognize that all colleagues do not interpret what they hear in the same way. Some of these involve paper-and-pencil exercises in which students answer a set of questions individually and then share and discuss their answers within a group of three to five of their colleagues. If the questions are written with any degree of ambiguity, groups will identify multiple meanings that were not evident to them when they read the questions individually.

Misinterpretation of language is a common theme used by some comic strip writers. Such comic strips provide an excellent vehicle for discussing the problem with students. For example, in one Adam comic strip, Brian Basset shows Adam cooking in the kitchen. In the same frame, his daughter, standing by his side, asks, "Daddy, may I please have a popsicle?" Adam replies, "Not this close to dinner." The next frame shows the child thinking, and in the next frame, she asks, "OK if I promise to eat it in the next room?"

The following two examples illustrate other approaches to this problem. In the first example, the purpose of the exercise appears to the student to be focused on the content of the course. The exercise involves showing a video clip to a class of life science students. The class is first shown a short video of a dancer performing. The class is then divided into groups of about four students each, and the instructor defines the task by telling the students to: "Describe what kind of information you would seek if you wanted to understand what is going on in her [the dancer's] body when she performs." The instruction is repeated, and the groups are given about 10 minutes to complete the task. Before proceeding with a discussion of the video designed to emphasize the integrative nature of physiology, biochemistry, and anatomy, each group is asked to describe their answer to the assigned task.

We have used this exercise with medical students on the first day of class, medical students in orientation workshops, and faculty in faculty development workshops. In one student workshop, six different descriptions of the task were elicited from eight groups of students. The responses ranged from "make a list of topics" to "design experiments and describe the kinds of measurements that you would make." Each student in the room heard the same words in the instructions spoken at the same time. Each student heard the words twice. Yet, the groups interpreted the words differently. The typical response of the students to this is surprise that there is such diversity in interpretation of a simple instruction, and they comment on the need to seek clarification if class members are to arrive at the same interpretation.

The second example also uses a video clip. In this case, the video clip shows a bird preening its feathers amid bleached logs and dune grass on a patch of sand. The soundtrack is that of an isolated ocean cove and includes the sound of waves and the sounds of gulls. The class is shown the video for 1 or 2 minutes. The students are then asked to describe the scene. They always respond that the video shows a bird preening itself. However, when asked where the bird is, three answers emerge. The bird is at the seashore because "I heard the waves." The bird is near a freeway because "I heard freeway noise." The bird is near an airport because "I heard planes taking off." When students answering "freeway" or "airport" are asked to explain the sounds of the gulls, they quickly respond that a garbage dump is nearby, and gulls live at the dump. The exercise gives these students first-hand knowledge of varied interpretations of information that all are receiving, and it reinforces the notion that their own colleagues do not necessarily see and hear what *they* see and hear. Thus, they come to realize the importance of seeking clarification within the context of this group of people.

Occasionally, a fourth answer to the question, "Where is the bird?" is voiced. This answer is that the bird is in a zoo rather than in the wild. When the student is pressed for the rationale underlying her or his answer, the response is that the scene was being viewed in school, and, "The teacher was trying to trick us!" This response shows the class that our past experience not only influences how we interpret what is said in class, but the context in which we are presented with the information influences our interpretation. This further emphasizes the need to seek clarification if any doubt about the message being delivered exists.

This simple exercise generates considerable discussion about the factors that influence interpretation of what is seen and heard. Upon completion of the exercise, students report that they had not realized how diverse interpretations of a seemingly simple scene can be. In addition, they voice a new appreciation for the need to seek clarification from colleagues and faculty when dealing with new information and new situations.

Creating a Safe Learning Environment

Students will not participate in an active learning environment if they do not feel safe doing so. Creating a safe learning environment is, perhaps, one of the biggest challenges facing faculty interested in creating an active learning environment. The challenge is not necessarily in knowing *what* to do to make the environment safe, it is in *doing* the things that promote safety. You must set the tone and model the behavior that you expect from the students. You must recognize that you are one member of a learning community (albeit a very prominent member), and that by exhibiting certain behavior, you, in essence, give permission to the other members of the community to behave in the same way. Thus, you must be willing to demonstrate vulnerability, demonstrate to students that you care about students' learning, admit to not knowing some things, be tolerant of questions, and be willing to seek clarification from the students.

ONE TEACHER'S EXPERIENCE IN CREATING A SAFE ENVIRONMENT

Establishing and maintaining a safe environment is a continuing process. Efforts must begin at the first meeting of the class and continue throughout the course. Although the exact path to establishing safety in the classroom depends, in large measure, on the individual instructor, the issues that the path must address are common to all classrooms. To explore these issues, let us first consider the steps that one instructor (HM) takes on the first day of class to begin to create a safe environment for his students. We will then discuss the rationale behind each of these steps.

A prominent feature of HM's classroom that students notice as the enter for the first time is the sound of music. Before class begins and during breaks, HM plays music. The genre changes as the course progresses in an attempt to ensure that each student will hear his or her preference in music at least once during the course, although hard rock, grunge, and hip-hop are not included in the mix. The rationale for playing music is that it may help create a safe learning environment. First, the music invites the student into the room. Instead of initially encountering the awkward silence that often characterizes a room full of potential strangers, the music provides a focus, and, in some cases, a topic for initiating conversation. It also provides a break between activities that have just been completed (e.g., a prior class) and the activities that are about to take place. Finally, it supplies a cue for the beginning of class. When the music is turned off, it is time for class to begin. Students respond positively to this practice and comment on its positive effects.

When the class period begins, each student is given two 3 × 5-inch index cards. One card is used for the "my job–your job" exercise described earlier. HM announces what the course is and asks the students to fill out this card. He then collects these cards and introduces himself to the class.

Before introducing himself, he sits on a lab stool at the front of the class. In the introduction, he tells the class that he has some personality flaws of which they should be aware. First, he has a terrific sense of humor that many people interpret as pure sarcasm, and in an attempt to be humorous, he sometimes says things that some people may interpret as being harsh and inappropriate. There is no intent to hurt anyone's feelings, and if this should happen, they should make sure to tell him so that he will be reminded to be more careful with his comments. The class is also told that in recent years, he has come to the conclusion that this behavior must be a genetic defect because it seems that more and more often when the family returns from an outing, his wife and daughter make comments to him that he remembers his mother telling his father when he was growing up.

HM continues the introduction by telling the students that he has a great interest in learning about how students think about science and how we can better help students learn science. He says that his job is to help the learner to learn and that in order to do this, he must know how students are thinking about things. The only way he can find this out is to ask them questions, and some of those questions may appear to the casual observer, but not necessarily to the person being asked, as condescending. He emphasizes that the act of being condescending requires intent, and that his intent is not to be condescending, but rather gain information about the questioner's thought process so that he can better meet the needs of the student asking the question. Furthermore, if anyone feels that HM has acted in a condescending manner, it is important that he or she talk with HM after class to help HM take steps to reduce the incidence of such occurrences.

After this introduction, HM continues with the "my job–your job" exercise. At the conclusion of the expectations discussion and a call for questions from the class, the students are asked to put their names on the second 3 × 5-inch index card and write anything that they think will (a) help HM learn more about them and (b) help HM to better help them learn. These cards are collected but not discussed in front of the class. The class continues with the exercises just described that are intended to help the students recognize the need to seek clarification.

Let us now review this first class period with an eye toward examining how HM's actions may promote a safe learning environment. When the students are first addressed in class, they are asked for their opinions about what will happen during the course. The first message that they receive is that the instructor is interested in what they think and that their opinions have some value to the instructor.

Before beginning a dialogue with the class, the instructor sits on a stool rather than standing in front of the class. The intent of this action is to create a more informal and comfortable atmosphere in the classroom. By sitting on a stool, the instructor symbolically places himself closer to the level of the student. The introduction becomes more of a conversation among equals rather than a lecture from an authority figure.

The introduction itself sends a valuable message to the students. It tells the student that the instructor is human with human frailties. Furthermore, the instructor recognizes these frailties and is not afraid to share them with the class. By doing so, he gives permission to the class to share their frailties. In addition, he defuses potential hostility that may result from comments that he may make. In announcing his personality flaws, he asks the students for understanding and tolerance. By asking for their understanding, he indicates that he will try to be understanding when interacting with students.

This message is also conveyed when he tells the students the purpose for the kind of questioning that may take place during class. This, along with the exercises emphasizing the diversity of interpretation of information, also suggests to the students that their learning may be enhanced if they begin to seek clarification from colleagues about their respective mental models.

The "my job–your job" discussion not only helps align expectations for the course, but it also provides an additional vehicle for conveying the message that the instructor cares about the students' learning. By telling the students that his job is to help the learner to learn and that he can't do that job without the students telling him what they need to learn, that is, to be willing to voice confusion, HM gives the students permission to ask what the students might think are "dumb" questions. The message conveyed to the students is that they cannot learn if they are not willing to admit confusion about the topics discussed.

Finally, the instructor tells the student that he is interested in them. He has told them a bit about himself, and he wants information about them. By providing them with the index cards, he has invited students to tell him anything about themselves that they feel will help him to understand their needs as students.

It should be clear that the efforts to make the classroom a safe environment do not end with the first-day activities. The messages of the first class must be reinforced throughout the duration of the class. Students need reassurance and reinforcement. They need to be told that learning is their responsibility and that they must take that responsibility seriously. For example, if the class discussion is going too slowly, they need to suggest that the discussion move on to the next topic. Similarly, if the class flow is too fast, they must raise their hands and suggest that the instructor summarize the major points of the discussion or, perhaps, slow the discussion. Whether the actual discussion moves on or slows is determined by a polling the class.

The communication begun with the "personal information" card can continue throughout the course in a variety of ways. For many instructors, e-mail provides a vehicle of this communication. Instructors encourage students to ask questions at any time via e-mail. Of course, the instructor must respond to these queries. A variation on this is to have students turn in 3×5-inch index cards at the beginning of class with a question, comment, or any other information that the student thinks the instructor should have. Responses to these can be given to the group at the beginning of the next class period, or they can be given to individual students via e-mail. It is important to recognize that if students are asked to engage in communication of this type, the instructor must respond in kind. This can take a significant amount of time, but, in general, the rewards are worth the effort.

How effective are these efforts to create a safe environment? Evaluations of the learning environment completed by students at the end of the quarter suggest that they are. In four classes where students (approximately 75 per class) were asked to respond on a five-point Likert scale (1=Strongly disagree, 3=Neutral, 5=Strongly agree) to the statement, "I felt that the learning environment was a safe environment in which I could raise any issue that concerned me," the average of the responses in the four classes ranged from 3.58 to 3.97.

SUMMARY

How do I get my students to "play the game?" The answer to the question is that you must make sure (a) that the students know what the rules of the game are; (b) that students recognize the need to seek clarification and the benefits of participation in terms of learning; and (c) that a safe learning environment in which students feel comfortable taking risks is established. It is important to recognize that reinforcement of these three factors is essential as the course progresses. Consistency within the framework of a safe learning environment cannot be overemphasized. Care must be taken that all members of the class, including the instructor, adhere to the "rules of the game."

With the appropriate preliminary steps and with an emphasis on maintaining a safe learning environment, students will be motivated to participate in an active learning environment. We can now consider different educational settings in which our job is to help the learner to learn and explore the variety of learning experiences that we can provide to help students move from the input state to the output state. In the next chapter, we will begin this exploration by considering the lecture hall venue.

Creating an Active Learning Environment in the Science Lecture Hall

CHAPTER OVERVIEW

The lecture hall is a physical environment that is optimized for the presentation of information by the instructor from the front of the room to an audience (the students), and lecturing is often an appropriate activity to meet the teacher's educational goals. However, it is essential that the lecturer recognize the need to engage the students in an active learning process. To accomplish this, the instructor must explicitly address a number of issues related to his or her role in the classroom and the educational goals that he or she has set for a given class session. A variety of techniques can be used to create an active learning environment in this physical setting. Each of them ultimately requires students (the learners) to test their current mental models of the phenomenon being considered. All of these techniques require the instructor to present challenges to the students' mental models and to present opportunities for the students to respond to those challenges. That is to say, all these techniques require an interaction between students and/or between students and the instructor. This chapter explores how the mindset of the instructor as a diagnostician and facilitator naturally leads to a variety of activities that promote active learning in this setting.

WHAT GOES ON IN THE TRADITIONAL LECTURE HALL?

The traditional *lecture hall* is a physical environment that has been optimized for the delivery of information by an instructor standing in the front to a class seated in a regular array throughout the room. Amphitheater-style lecture halls with steeply arranged ranks of seats are designed to make the unamplified voice of the lecturer clearly audible to every member of the audience. Add a blackboard (these days, a white board), a projection screen, and slide, overhead, and video projectors, and you have an environment in which information (auditory and visual) readily flows from the front of the room to the furthest corners of the lecture hall.

BEFORE PROCEEDING!

Consider for a moment your own experiences in a traditional lecture setting. What problems have you encountered as a member of the audience in such a setting? What problems do you think your students encounter in a similar environment?

The traditional *lecture,* regardless of the physical setting in which it occurs, is intended to deliver information to the students assembled in the room, and it is assumed that if information is delivered, it is "learned" by those students. The teacher's focus is on the class as a whole, rarely on the individual student. Interactions between the teacher and individual students are thus constrained, possibly by the physical setting, and certainly by the teacher's intentions. The size of the class, the number of students in the room, is not the issue here. We are concerned with the teacher's goals.

WHAT ARE THE GOALS OF THE TEACHER?

We must begin with the assumption that the overall goal of the teacher is to help the learner to learn. Thus, when the teacher intends to deliver information, when this is the most appropriate learning experience to help the learner to learn, there are other objectives that must also be pursued. The teacher must foster an active learning environment, promoting each student's engagement with his or her own developing mental model(s) of the subject under consideration. Further, the teacher must always determine the input and output states of the students as he or she lectures; where are they when I start and where did they get to when I have finished? Are the students "getting the message?" Are their mental models correct or are misconceptions creeping in? So, when lecturing, the teacher has many things to accomplish.

WHAT ARE THE LIMITATIONS OF THE TRADITIONAL LECTURE AND LECTURE HALL?

A presumably unintended consequence of the physical arrangement of almost all lecture venues (whether traditional amphitheaters or more ordinary classrooms) is the fact that the acoustics often make it very difficult for the lecturer in the front of the hall to hear questions or answers voiced by members of the class. It is also difficult for other members of the class to hear a comment made by a colleague seated in their midst.

This functional asymmetry (information flows relatively easily from front to back and quite poorly from back to front or from side to side) certainly contributes to, but is not the sole cause of, the passivity with which most students listen to a lecture, however stimulating and entertaining.

If you recognize the need to engage the students in an active learning process, there are a number of different approaches to accomplishing this (to be described later in this chapter). However, to be successful, you will need to explicitly address a number of issues related to your role in the classroom and the educational goals that you have set for a given class session.

CREATING AN ACTIVE LEARNING ENVIRONMENT IN THE LECTURE HALL

You can use a variety of techniques to create an active learning environment in a lecture setting. Each of them ultimately requires students (the learners) to test their current mental models of the phenomenon being considered. All of these techniques require that you present challenges to the students' mental models. You must also provide opportunities for the students to respond to these challenges. That is to say, all these techniques require an interaction between students and/or between you and your students. Such interactions not only facilitate the students' building more robust, correct mental models, but they make it possible for you to continuously diagnose the learning state (input and output states) of the class.

BEFORE PROCEEDING!

What can you do to help your students become more active learners when you lecture? What can you do to get students to "play the game" that you want played?

The fundamental feature of an active learning lecture is presenting a challenge to the students' mental models. This almost always takes the form of a question or problem addressed to the class. However, unlike what happens in all too many classrooms, you must actually give students time to attempt to answer the question! It is now well known that teachers habitually wait less than 1 second before answering their own questions or at least pushing the discussion forward (Rowe, 1974). This occurs, at least in part, because students are reluctant to volunteer an answer to a question posed by the teacher. Equally important, too many teachers view a longer pause for an answer as a waste of "valuable" time in which additional content could be dispensed. However, it is also clear that extending the "wait time" after a question to as little as 3 seconds has significant effects on student behavior (their responses get "better" and they ask more questions; Tobin & Capie, 1980).

So, let us begin by considering some approaches to structuring interactions between you and your students. We will then turn to a consideration of the many ways you can challenge (question) the class.

A number of quite similar approaches to making the lecture setting an opportunity for active learning have been described by science educators: *think-pair-share* (Kagan & Kagan, 1994), *peer instruction* (Mazur, 1997), and *nearest neighbor* problem solving (Michael & Rovick, 1999). For these to be most productive, students must feel that the class setting is a safe one where they can feel free to volunteer answers even when they might be wrong. In Chapter 7 we discussed some ways in which the teacher can create this essential feeling of safety.

In the *think-pair-share* paradigm a question is posed for the class and the students are asked to first individually generate an answer (often written) to the question and then turn to a neighbor and discuss their answers and agree on a joint answer. The teacher then solicits representative answers from the class.

Peer instruction, as implemented by Mazur (1997) in his physics classroom, involves a very similar protocol. A lecture is interspersed with concept-based questions. Each student is asked to select an answer for the question and then convince a neighbor that her or his answer is correct.

The *nearest neighbor* paradigm described by Michael and Rovick (1999) generates a very similar interaction between students. A problem is put to the class and students are asked to work with a small group of neighbors to solve the problem. The class is given a few minutes, and then answers are solicited and discussed by the entire class.

How do you choose which of these three approaches you adopt for your classroom? They are, after all, very similar. The best answer is to use the one you are most comfortable with or that seems to work best with your students.

> ## BEFORE PROCEEDING!
>
> Think about the characteristics that the three approaches described above have in common. How might these features be incorporated in your classroom activities?

The similarities between these three approaches to active learning in the lecture hall are obvious. In each, a problem or question is posed to the class that challenges each student's mental model. Students are given an opportunity to work together to solve the problem or answer the question. Interaction with their peers usually requires each student to articulate his or her understanding or generate an explanation for their chosen approach to solving the problem. These processes of self-explanation (Chi et. al, 1994) and peer or reciprocal teaching (Brown & Palinscar , 1989) are known to lead to gains in understanding, i.e., to better and more robust mental models. Furthermore, these interactions require students to actually use the language of the discipline to construct an explanation, and facility with the language of a discipline has long been regarded as a part of attaining mastery of that subject matter (Frawley, 1988; Lemke, 1990).

When students work in groups or pairs in this way, it is very much easier to get them to volunteer answers than when each student is working alone; when their group is correct, each student can take "credit" for the correct answer, but when they are wrong, they seem to feel that only some of the "blame" belongs to them.

Once answers have been elicited, they can be discussed by you and by other members of the class. Further, such a discussion presents an ideal opportunity for you to model the kind of problem-solving process that you want the students to practice.

This interaction also provides you with a great deal of information about the "state" of the students, helping to define what they know and what they don't know. Equally important, it makes "visible" to you how the students are thinking about the particular topic being considered. This kind of interaction thus facilitates your job as a diagnostician (see chap. 5), providing important information on which to base the next educational experience (provide another problem, review the topic immediately at hand, go back and review a still earlier topic that apparently was not mastered, move on to the next topic, help the students recognize the consequences of their faulty thinking or misconceptions).

HOW CAN WE CHALLENGE THE STUDENTS' MENTAL MODELS IN THE LECTURE HALL?

Any thoughtful question can represent a challenge to the students' mental models of the phenomenon being discussed. You can ask questions about novel (previously undiscussed) situations, external disturbances to the system, or the consequences of changes to the system. Such questions seem to fall into a few broad categories (see Table 8.1): questions about qualitative changes, questions calling for (semi-) quantitative answers, and questions requiring the students to reason about something. Such questions can be used to assess the students' input or output states.

Qualitative prediction questions generally take one of two forms. Given the chemical reaction $A + B \rightleftharpoons C + D$, if the concentration of A increases, what will happen to the concentration of D? In this example, a single variable was changed, and the students were asked to predict the qualitative change to another variable. However, another form of qualitative prediction questions starts by describing a change to the system itself and asks what the consequences will be. For example, if the heart is denervated, what change, if any, will occur to heart rate (will it increase, decrease, or stay the same)?

In the lecture setting, challenges to the students' mental models do not usually take the form of questions requiring exact mathematical calculation (although Michael and Rovick, 1999, do use their nearest neighbor paradigm for quantitative problem solving). However, it is common to ask students questions requiring **quantitative thinking** to arrive at an answer. Table 8.2 contains an example of such a problem from Mazur (1997). Obviously, a question like this could be displayed with an overhead projector and the students asked to select an answer, or the stem of the question could be presented and students asked to volunteer an answer.

TABLE 8.1

Types of challenges to students' mental models

1. Predict changes to system (*qualitative*)
    A. If the value of X changes, how will the value of Y change?
    B. If the system is "changed" (its structure or overall properties), how will the value of X change?
2. Predict changes to system (*semi-quantitative*). What will happen to X if Y doubles?
3. Given a situation described by X, Y, and Z, what would you expect to "see" (*reason about*) in terms of A and B?

TABLE 8.2

A classroom problem requiring quantitative reasoning

A constant force is exerted on a cart that is initially at rest on an air track. Friction between the cart and the track is negligible. The force acts for a short time interval and gives the cart a certain final speed. To reach the same final speed with a force that is only half as big, the force must be exerted on the cart for a time interval _____ that for the stronger force.

1. four times as long as
2. twice as long as
3. equal to
4. half as long as
5. a quarter of

Note: From Mazur, 1997.

Finally, questions can require the students to reason about some situation, perhaps a novel one that they have not yet encountered. For example, here is a problem that might be presented in an earth science or geology classroom (from Tarbuck & Lutgens, 2000): "Describe the consequences that a great and prolonged increase in explosive volcanic activity might have on each of the Earth's four spheres."

ASKING QUESTIONS IN A WAY
THAT ENGAGES THE STUDENTS

There are many ways in which students in the lecture hall can be challenged to think about their mental models. Any question requiring thinking posed to the students during a lecture can help the students determine whether they understand the subject under discussion and help the lecturer determine whether what he or she is doing is helping the learner to learn.

There are two other approaches to creating an active learning environment in the lecture hall that deserve mention: the use of "props" and student participation in role-playing activities.

Many science concepts can be demonstrated or illuminated by having students interact with simple physical systems. For example, if the topic of the lecture involves elastic structures (whether encountered in physiology or physics), you can give balloons to the students and allow them a few minutes to explore some of the more obvious phenomena associated with the property of elastic recoil. Breathing through straws of different size or length can create opportunities for extending the students' understanding of resistance to flow. Pop beads can be used to let students build proteins from amino acids or assemble RNA or DNA molecules. Use your imagination to identify simple things that can be used to explore the concepts of any particular science discipline.

Bear in mind, however, that the goal here is active "heads," not simply active hands! Playing with balloons can help students understand elastic recoil if the students are given a task, a question to answer or a problem to solve, that will cause them to challenge their own mental models of the phenomenon. On the other hand, random play, while perhaps diverting and fun, is not likely to lead to any significant insights about elastic structures like lungs or steel beams.

Another way to promote model building and testing in the lecture hall is to engage students in role-playing activities that illustrate ("dramatize") important phenomena. Modell (in Modell & Carroll, 1993) has described an activity in which one individual assumes the role of the normal cardiac pacemaker (the sinoatrial node). A second individual assumes the role of another pacemaker with a slower intrinsic rate (the atrioventricular node), and a third person plays a third pacemaker cell with an even slower intrinsic rate (Purkije system cell). Changes in the behavior of the sinoatrial or atrioventriclar node "cells" being modeled will lead to responses that closely mimic important changes in the function of the heart.

It is important when using such role-playing games that you involve not only the "actors" but all members of the class. One way to do this is to ask students in the audience to predict the changes in behavior that will result from changing the properties of one of the cells. Another is to involve members of the class in suggesting changes in the properties of the three cells. In this activity, the whole class is involved because it monitors the actions of the "actors" and provides feedback to them if their responses are not correct.

THE ROLE OF TECHNOLOGY IN THE LECTURE HALL

How can technology be used in the lecture hall to help the learner to learn and promote meaningful learning?

BEFORE PROCEEDING!

What technology do you use when you lecture? Why do you use that particular technology? What does it enable you to do? What drawbacks does it have? How do the benefits and costs affect student learning?

Before we can answer this question we must be sure we know what technology we are discussing. Most often when we use this term we are thinking of computers, CD-ROMs or video projectors, and these certainly are forms of technology. However, it is important to keep in mind that everything we use in learning and teaching—the lecture hall itself, the white board, the slide projector, textbooks—embodies a technology. And every technology enables us to do some things (or makes some things easier to do) but at the same time may make other things more difficult. Thus, it is important that we make decisions about the technologies we will employ based on a careful weighing of the pluses and minuses of each, and on our goals for the experience.

So what guidelines can we establish for using any technology in the lecture setting? Our rule of thumb is that we use one form of technology when that technology offers us something that can't be achieved with less complicated forms of technology. When using the blackboard or whiteboard will enable us to illustrate an important phenomenon or present a simple graph to make a point, we will use that technology. On the other hand, if we need to display a photomicrograph of a tissue section or a mineral section, a slide projector will enable us to provide the vital visual image that is needed. If, however, we want our students to think about the behavior of a system, a computer simulation or animation projected on the screen may provide the only way to accomplish this. There must always be a match between the technology and the task at hand.

Let's focus, then, on how you might use the "high technologies" of the computer, CD-ROM, and video projectors in the lecture hall setting.

More and more lecture venues have been equipped with computers and video projectors. This, coupled with the ready availability of presentation programs (PowerPoint® is perhaps the most common example), has led to increasing numbers of lectures delivered with the aid of the computer. While there are several advantages to this technology (ease of modifying the content from year to year or even from day to day), there are also some associated "costs." For example, computer "bugs" (whether hardware or software) or operator error can easily create situations in which the interactions you are trying to foster with your students are interrupted. Furthermore, the very ease of putting up words and images on the screen can foster a situation of information overload for the students.

A limitation of PowerPoint® and most other presentation programs is the inability to modify a slide "on the fly" during your lecture. On the other hand, this is easily done when you use transparencies on an overhead projector. You can also create transparencies as you lecture, often a desirable way to help students organize their own models of the phenomena you are discussing.

These are not arguments against using PowerPoint® presentations, merely cautionary notes, reminders, that any technology has pluses and minuses that you must think about.

While "slides" (whether photographic, or transparencies, or computer generated) make it possible to project static images in full color, they will not serve to make visible phenomena that change in time and/or space. However, the computer can provide an opportunity to use animations in class, and the availability of animations is increasing as textbook publishers produce CD-ROMs to accompany textbooks in most areas of science and as the number of animations available over the Internet increases.

Animations can be used to demonstrate a concept. For example, an animation of actin and myosin interaction in skeletal muscle may provide a visualization of events that otherwise cannot easily be seen, or even understood, from static pictures. Another example of this application is an animation of a chemical reaction. However, students viewing a computer animation may not be any more active mentally than when they view their favorite television program. The power of an animation to aid student learning is a function of the extent to which this technology is embedded in a context that causes the students to test their mental models of the phenomena being examined.

Here's an example of what we mean. A widely distributed CD-ROM that accompanies an introductory anatomy and physiology text includes an animation of the events that occur when a needle is inserted through the chest wall into the intrapleural space. The result is that the intrapleural pressure (the pressure in the virtual space between the inside of the chest wall and the outside of the lung) equilibrates with atmospheric pressure. As a consequence, the coupling of the lung and chest wall is broken, the lung recoils to a smaller volume, and the chest wall recoils to a larger volume. A narrative accompanies the animation that describes the events that occur in this pneumothorax. The intent of the *author* is to simply present this information to the student.

However, this animation can be used to help students test their mental model of the mechanical interaction of the lung and chest wall. To use it in this way, the instructor describes an experiment to the class (e.g., a needle is inserted through the chest wall into the intrapleural space). The class is then given the task of predicting what will happen to lung volume and chest wall volume as a consequence of inserting the needle. After discussing the predictions made by members of the class, the instructor shows the remainder of the animation (with or without the accompanying audio). When used this way, the instructor has employed the animation as an experiment. This same technique could be used with video clips of actual experiments, computer simulations, and the growing number of on-line experiments available on the Internet.

All of the technologies that are now available to us wherever it is we lecture can contribute to creating a learning environment in which the students are continuously challenged to build and test their mental models. The task becomes choosing the technology that provides you with the best opportunity to help your students reach your output state goals.

Our discussion of using technology has been focused on the classroom. However, the technology available through the World Wide Web and the Internet offers opportunities to extend the active learning environment beyond the classroom. The Web offers a source for a vast amount of information. However, this access is not where the power of the technology lies for enhancing the learning environment of the lecture hall. The power lies in the extent to which communication can be increased among students and between the instructor and students. The instructor can use a web site to provide students with additional problems, solutions, and updated information related to the course. Discussion forums, Listserves, and e-mail allow classroom discussion to continue after the formal class period has ended. These vehicles also provide a certain degree of safety for the discussants beyond that offered in the classroom. Thus, this technology can bring a new dimension to the learning environment. This potential is not limited to the lecture hall. It can be equally beneficial in the conference room setting. We will discuss this setting in the next chapter.

9

Promoting Active Learning in the "Conference Room"

CHAPTER OVERVIEW

We define the "conference room" as a setting in which (relatively) small numbers of students interact with each other and with the instructor. What is needed here are challenges to the students' mental models. Most frequently this is done by providing problems that are to be solved. This also provides an opportunity for instructors to model the kinds of problem-solving behaviors that they want the students to master. It is an environment in which the instructor can provide as much or as little help as circumstances require and can provide the most timely and appropriate feedback to the students.

We define the "conference room" as a setting (which may or may not be physically distinct from the space in which lectures are delivered or lab experiments are carried out) in which every student in a relatively small group of students can potentially interact with each other and with the instructor (Michael, 1993; Michael & Rovick, 1999). Along with lectures and/or laboratories, science courses commonly include sessions variously described as "discussion sections," "problem-solving sessions," "workshops," or perhaps "lab discussion sections." The issue to be confronted here is how to create an active learning environment for students in such sessions.

WHAT GOES ON IN THE CONFERENCE ROOM?

Before dealing with implementation issues, it is important to establish what the educational objectives are for such small group sessions. In general, small group sessions are intended to help students learn to "do" something with the information that they have already acquired. They are not usually intended as a forum for the dissemination, or acquisition, of new knowledge, although it is to be expected that students *will* learn new knowledge as they attempt to solve problems and discover that they do not have information essential for the task at hand. If this is the case, then, the teacher's traditional role in the classroom must be reassessed. What is required here is a quite different approach to helping the learner to learn than is employed in the lecture setting. What remains constant is the need to assess the input and output states of the students.

What sorts of things should students be learning to "do" in small group sessions? There are often two broad goals for such sessions: (a) assisting students to **integrate information** into bigger, more accurate and more robust mental models, and (b) helping them learn to **apply knowledge** to the solution of problems (see chap. 2). These goals are generally pursued through instructor modeling of the desired behaviors and student practice of these behaviors with appropriate feedback.

Let's consider in more detail the various things that are at work in the conference setting. You and the students are confronted with problems to be solved. This affords you with an opportunity to demonstrate or model how problems are to be solved. In solving such problems you can demonstrate (model) the use of many pieces of information and the integration of these pieces into a whole with which to solve the problem. You also will be demonstrating the use of the language of some particular science discipline as information is marshaled, integrated, and then used in some reasoning process to arrive at an answer. An important, aspect of the process is sharing the rationale behind your approach to the problem.

When it is the students' turn to solve problems, similar things happen. Students will have to assemble the knowledge needed to solve the problem (from their own memory, from textbooks, from other students in their group) and put it together. Students will have to practice speaking the language of the discipline with each other and with the teacher. The students will also be practicing solving the particular problems that have been assigned, and they can receive feedback about their solutions from their peers and from you.

As the students do this, you, in your role of diagnostician, can determine what mental models the students are using, how accurate and appropriate those models are, and how well they can employ the particular problem-solving skills that need to be employed.

The conference room is an environment in which you can provide as much or as little help as circumstances require and can provide the most timely and appropriate feedback to the students.

What Should Be Discussed in These Sessions?

Traditionally in science courses, discussion sections have either dealt with the results obtained in student laboratories or they have dealt with "problems" either assigned as homework or assigned to be done in the discussion section.

Laboratory discussions will be considered in detail in Chapter 10, but the ideas being developed here are certainly applicable to that setting. In brief, what is most important is that the students confront their mental models for the phenomena they explored in the laboratory, consider the predictions they made about expected outcomes, compare the actual results to their predictions, and finally use any differences between what they expected and what they observed to drive a process of mental model building or rebuilding.

Problem-solving sessions offer the maximum flexibility in that any kind of problem can serve as the basis for a fruitful interaction between students and between teacher and students.

Obviously you must pick problems that match the educational objectives you have set for your students in terms of subject matter, problem-solving skills to be exercised (whether qualitative or quantitative reasoning, requiring analysis or synthesis), and degree of difficulty.

BEFORE PROCEEDING!

What problems would you ask your students to solve?
Why did you pick the problems you did?

Furthermore, problems should be "interesting" to the students. This often means identifying problems to which students are most likely to be able to personally relate. For example, students in a physiology or biology course are interested in the functioning of their own bodies and hence a topic such as exercise is likely to hold the attention of students. "Clinical" problems also have great attraction, even when the focus of the problem is not in any sense really medical. Everyone has a relative or friend with a problem such as heart failure, diabetes, or asthma. Other problems that students in a biology course can easily relate to can be taken from the realm of environmental issues (pesticides as pseudo-hormones, the consequences of water or air pollution). Students in earth science or geology courses are likely to be interested in natural disasters (volcanic eruptions, earthquakes, etc.), particularly when stories about such events have recently been in the news. Chemistry students can be easily motivated to solve problems about environmental problems (acid rain, PCBs) or problems involving everyday activities (cooking) or objects (plastics).

If confrontation with a problem is to succeed in helping students integrate information and develop important problem-solving skills, it is necessary that the problem require more than simple recollection or acquisition of some piece of knowledge (the exercise should NOT be a "Trivial Pursuit"® game with science as the category). The problem must be complex enough to require the solver to marshal many pieces of information, concepts, or relationships. Furthermore, solving the problem should require the student to "do" something with the information or knowledge when it is identified as being relevant. This might involve generating causal diagrams, concept maps, or other visual organizers, calculating the value of certain system parameters, diagnosing (identifying the cause of) some particular process occurring, or explaining what is happening in a system. Tables 2.2 and 2.3 contain examples of the kinds of problems that might be used in a "conference room" problem-solving session. Table 9.1 contains an example of a problem to be solved over a number of discussion sessions (after confronting the data presented in the first session, students have the opportunity to begin the solution to the problem before considering additional data in a second session).

MAKING YOUR CONFERENCES
AN ACTIVE LEARNING EXPERIENCE

Conferences are meant to be sessions in which the students interact with one another and with the teacher. The success of such sessions will be strongly influenced by the physical environment in which the session occurs, as well as the way in which these interactions are managed.

BEFORE PROCEEDING!

Consider where you hold conferences and what it is you arrange for your students to do in these sessions. What problems have you encountered in making these sessions successful? What would you change if you could?

Although the lecture hall is built so that all eyes are on the lecturer and sound travels best from front to back, the conference setting should allow for

TABLE 9.1

An example of a multi-session discussion problem

Session 1

Ms. A. C. is a 44-year old lawyer who was referred to a physician by her dentist, who noted hyperpigmentation of her gums. In any case, she had been meaning to see a doctor because of weakness, fatigue, and lightheadedness. She also stated that she read an article in a magazine that convinced her that she was suffering from hypoglycemia: she develops a rapid heartbeat, shakiness, sweating, and faintness if she does not eat promptly on arising in the morning or if she misses a meal. These symptoms are relieved 15 to 20 minutes after eating. It is January in Chicago, yet the patient, who has not traveled, looks as though she had just returned from a vacation in the Caribbean. Laboratory tests were performed but the results are not yet available.

Describe a mechanism to account for each of the patient's symptoms.

Is there a single abnormality that could give rise to all her symptoms? Explain.

Session 2

Lab test results are shown below.

TEST	RESULT
plasma $[Na^+]$	132 mM
plasma $[K^+]$	5.2 mM
fasting blood glucose	60 mg/dl
morning plasma [ACTH]	148 pg/ml
morning plasma [cortisol]	6 µg/dl

Do these lab results support your hypothesized mechanism(s) giving rise to the patient's symptoms?

What's wrong with Ms. A. C.? Explain.

Note: Modified from Michael & Rovick, 1999.

eye contact between all students and for easy verbal exchanges between all students. Tables that will accommodate small groups of students work well. If standard student chairs (with arms) are available, they can be arranged in small circles to facilitate communications. Long tables do not work as well since eye contact and communication between all participants are harder to maintain. It is important to arrange the furniture (if that is possible) so that you can easily circulate among the groups at work in the room and so the students can get to the board or the overhead projector to post answers.

Obviously, you will have to work with the rooms to which you are assigned and the furniture that is available there. However, regardless of the space constraints, paying attention to maximizing the opportunity for interaction will have an immediate payoff in terms of the success of your sessions.

To make conference sessions interactive it is important that small groups of students (3–6) work together at whatever the assigned task might be. Groups can be allowed to form spontaneously. However, this may lead to groups that are too large for sustained interaction or to individuals working alone. Both should be discouraged as forcefully as possible. An alternative approach is for you to assign individuals to groups. This can be done at random at the time of the session ("count off 1 to 5 and all the 1's form a group") or groups can be formed ahead of time, mixing genders and achievement levels, etc. You can assign students to a group for the entire academic term or group assignments can be changed at desired intervals.

An important issue is whether the students are assigned problems prior to the discussion session or whether the problems are identified for the students only when they arrive at the session. If the goal is to maximize student–student interaction (peer learning), it is most effective if all students solve the problem together in class. When students are assigned the problems as homework, the level of preparation will vary widely, there will be less peer teaching, and less interaction of any kind between the students.

Instructor modeling of the solution to a problem, or piece of a problem, requires more that simply writing down the relevant equation, plugging in the appropriate values for the variables, and carrying out the required math. Modeling requires you to explain your reasoning process in some detail, explaining what led to the selection of the appropriate equation, how the relevant data was identified, and what the results mean when obtained. Michael and Rovick (1999) have provided quite detailed answers to the problems they have published so as to provide students with a model of how to think about the problems.

This modeling should not be done as a lecture, with you talking and the students listening. Rather, it should be carried out in as interactive a fashion as possible. Questions and hints can be used to assist the students in proposing the next step or the next piece of information required. In this way, you develop the required solution with the active assistance of the students.

When it is the students' turn to solve a problem, it is useful to have each group publically display, or post, the answer arrived at by their group. This can be done in a variety of ways: each group can be given a transparency on which to write, answers can be posted on a transparency that you have produced, or answers can be written on large pieces of paper taped to the wall or on the blackboard. The benefits of such public display are twofold. First, it makes it easy to compare and contrast answers from each group. This then provides a useful starting point for the whole group discussion that will ensue. Another benefit of such public display is that each group feels some "ownership" of their answer and encourages them to explain or defend their work during the discussion.

WHAT IS THE ROLE OF THE INSTRUCTOR IN DISCUSSION SESSIONS?

We have already discussed the importance of the teacher modeling the problem solving that should be done. When the students are working in their small groups to solve the problem, you should be circulating among the groups to facilitate the work of each group. This may call for answering a question from a group, making a suggestion or giving a hint based on what you hear in the group's conversation, or it may require helping each group interact most effectively (getting silent students to contribute, getting very vocal students to let others contribute).

While facilitating the work of the groups, you are also learning a great deal about the state of the students. The conversations heard will tell you what problems the students are having, what misconceptions are present, what knowledge is available to the students, what seems to be missing, etc. It is this information that you will need to use in the next interaction with either individual groups or with the whole group (see chap. 3 for a discussion of our model for any learning experience).

Finally, it is essential that you create an environment in which each student participates to the fullest possible extent. This requires that the students know the "rules of the game" and understand what it is they are supposed to do in this setting (how they are to behave). They must also feel "safe" in the learning environment (see chap. 7).

The students can only know the "rules of the game" if you clearly and explicitly communicate them. It is also essential that you play by the same rules at all times. This means that when it comes time for formal student assessment, the test used corresponds to what was said to be important in the discussion section. However often you tell your students that they will need to learn problem solving in the discussion sections, if all you test is their ability to regurgitate memorized information, you will lose your credibility, and your students will make little effort to learn to solve problems.

A feeling of safety requires that students feel free to ask questions without fear of a "penalty" (public humiliation, two points off their grade). Students must feel free to answer a question, knowing that there will be no cost to them if they are wrong. Students must feel that their contribution to the discussion is not only expected, but it is valued. In order to create such an environment it essential that you, the teacher, model the kinds of behaviors you expect from your students and that you hold all of your students to the behaviors that you expect.

Chapter

10

Helping the Learner to Learn in the Student Laboratory

CHAPTER OVERVIEW

Student laboratories are thought to provide an active learning environment in which students can build robust mental models of important phenomena. However, the usual laboratory protocol functions as little more than a recipe for "doing things" without necessarily encouraging the students to "think about" what they are doing. Easily implemented changes in the way in which these labs are conducted can have very large effects on student model building and repair.

WHAT ARE THE GOALS OF YOUR STUDENT LABORATORIES?

If your job is helping the learner to learn science, what should you have your students do in the student laboratory? What tasks should you set for the students? How should they pursue the completion of those tasks? What kinds of behaviors do you expect of them? And how should you facilitate the processes that go on in the laboratory?

The answers to these questions obviously depend on what it is you expect your students to take away from their experiences there, what your output state goals are:

- One common goal of laboratories is to allow students to demonstrate for themselves important phenomena from the discipline being studied. It is thought that this will help students build their own mental models from the information they have accumulated. This, in turn, should result in a more robust understanding or increased meaningful learning in the discipline.

- Another goal might be to give students experience actually using the tools of science, whether to increase their appreciation of what scientists do and how they do it, or to prepare students to actually work in a laboratory (whether commercial, academic, or in a health environment).
- Finally, laboratories can be designed to allow students to "do" science in much the same way that scientists "do" science. In this case the intent is to give students experience actually applying the "scientific method" to the solving of some problem.

We will be concerned here mainly with the issue of helping students to approach their activities in the laboratory in a way that will maximize meaningful learning or understanding of the discipline. That said, our suggestions are certainly applicable to helping students accomplish the other two goals just described.

THE PROBLEMS OF TRADITIONAL STUDENT LABORATORIES

Students generally go into the laboratory only after attending lectures and doing the assigned reading about some topic. The assumption, then, is that the students have accumulated a set of facts before they go into the laboratory. However, it is important to recognize that we rarely test this assumption in any way, and as a consequence we do not know the input state of the students when they begin a laboratory exercise.

In physics, chemistry, some areas of biology, and many other science courses, laboratory "experiments" are usually designed to demonstrate certain phenomena to the student. Experiments are designed so that students will be as active as possible (e.g., they do as much as possible themselves). The desired outcome is for the students to be able to describe how the underlying principles or concepts lead to the phenomena that they demonstrated for themselves. If they succeed at this, it is assumed that the students have increased their understanding of the phenomena, that they have achieved some level of meaningful learning.

From the students' view, however, the lab experience may be nothing more than a series of steps to be carried out with the eventual outcome being "data." If "wrong" answers (data) are obtained, something "didn't work," and the results are often discarded. Since the students "know" the "correct" answer (e.g., they know what they should have seen), they can generate perfectly correct explanations for phenomena they never demonstrated.

Under these circumstances, are your students testing their current mental models, or are your students merely collecting data? In most student laboratories, the latter best describes what happens. If your job is to help the learner to learn, how can you change the laboratory experience so that students do test and modify their mental models?

CREATING AN ACTIVE LABORATORY EXPERIENCE

The key to helping the learner test and refine his or her mental model in the laboratory setting lies in how you direct your students to behave in the laboratory. That is, the directions you give to the student (the lab write-up or protocol) will determine what kind of learning occurs.

Several years ago, as part of a faculty development workshop, we ran an informal experiment to see if the lab protocol design influenced the "students'" behavior and perception of a lab experience (Modell, 1991). The attendees of the workshop (the "students") included physiologists, biomedical engineers, medical clinicians, and a few administrative personnel. The laboratory exercise was based on a Mr. Wizard exercise for creating a reed instrument from a drinking straw (Herbert, 1965).

The "class" was divided into five lab groups of four or five "students" each. Three lab groups were given the protocol shown in Figure 10.1 (the "cookbook" protocol). Notice that this protocol, which is similar in format to "traditional" lab protocols directing students in biology, physics, chemistry, and many other science classes, tells the student to "do this," "record this," "tell me what you saw," and, in some cases, "interpret what you saw." This protocol does not explicitly encourage students to test their mental models about the phenomena being examined.

The remaining two groups were given the alternative protocol shown in Figure 10.2. Notice that this protocol directs the students to explain their observations as they were making them, asks them to address questions related to the principles involved as they are conducting the experiment, and asks them to make predictions about what they think will happen during the experiment.

During the 15–20 minute time period allotted to the exercise, the instructor interacted with one of the cookbook protocol groups by asking group members questions about their observations and how they interpreted their results, and by asking them to predict the results of the subsequent steps in the protocol. No interaction of this type was attempted with any of the other groups.

Following the exercise, each group was asked how they approached the laboratory. The two cookbook groups (Fig. 10.1) that did not interact with the instructor followed the protocol steps in order with very little group interaction. Each group member worked with his or her own straw and followed the steps without giving much thought to the underlying principles.

SOUND LABORATORY (A)

Objective: To explore the mechanism of sound production in woodwind instruments.

Materials: Several drinking straws, scissors

Procedure:

1.   Pinch one end of a drinking straw for about 3/4 of an inch from the end. Blow gently through the straw. Record what you hear on the data table below.
2.   Cut the corners of the flat end of the straw off diagonally with the scissors (see illustration). Now blow gently through the "reeds" that you've made so that the "reeds" vibrate. It takes a little practice to find out how hard to blow and how to adjust the "reed" with your lips to vibrate it. Record what you hear on the data table below.
3.   Shorten the length of the straw by cutting a 2-inch piece off of the non-reed end. Blow your "instrument" again. Compare the pitch of the sound to the previous trial. Repeat this experiment.
4.   Make a second "instrument." In this straw, cut a finger hole about 2 inches from the non-reed end, and cut a second finger hole about 4 inches from the non-reed end. Blow the instrument first with the finger holes covered and then with each of the finger holes open. Compare the note obtained with both finger holes open to that obtained from the shorter instrument from step 3.

Questions:

1.   Why wasn't a sound produced when you blew on the original straw?
2.   What happened to the air in the straw when the "reeds" vibrated?
3.   Is it the vibrating "reeds" or the vibrating air column that makes the sound coming from your "instrument?"
4.   What effect did opening the finger holes have on the column of air in the instrument?

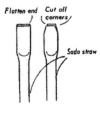

DATA TABLE	
Instrument design	Sound produced
Straw with pinched end	
Full length straw with reeds	
Straw with reeds shortened by 2"	
Straw with reeds shortened by 4"	
Straw with reeds and finger holes	

FIG 10.1.   The cookbook protocol. From Herbert, D. (1965). *Mr. Wizards's science secrets.* **New York: Hawthorn Books, Inc.**

When these groups reached the questions, they did not readily connect what they had done in the experiment with the questions. This response was interesting because these "students" were, in fact, experienced, practicing scientists. Yet, when placed in a student mode, their behavior was similar to students attending a lab course. Their goal was to complete the exercise in the shortest possible time, obtaining the prescribed data without paying too much attention to the factors that determined the data.

The groups with the alternative protocol (Fig. 10.2) approached the exercise in an entirely different manner. Each group member worked with his or her own straws much as the cookbook group members did. However, members of the al-

SOUND LABORATORY (B)

Objective: To explore the mechanism of sound production in woodwind instruments.

Materials: Several drinking straws, scissors

Procedure:

1.   Pinch one end of a drinking straw for about 3/4 of an inch from the end. Blow gently through the straw. Was a sound (a "note") produced by blowing through the straw? Is that what you would have predicted? Why?

2.   Cut the corners of the flat end of the straw off diagonally with the scissors (see illustration). Now blow gently through the "reeds" that you've made so that the "reeds" vibrate. It takes a little practice to find out how hard to blow and how to adjust the "reed" with your lips to vibrate it. What happens to the column of air in the straw when the "reeds" vibrate? What do you hear when the reeds vibrate?

3.   Is it the vibrating "reeds" or the vibrating air column that makes the sound coming from your "instrument?" Shorten the length of the straw by cutting a 2-inch piece off of the non-reed end. Blow your "instrument" again. What have you done to the "reeds?" What has happened to the air column? Compare the pitch of the sound to the previous trial. What would happen if you shorten the straw again? Repeat this experiment. Was your prediction correct?

4.   Can the air column be shortened without shortening the straw? Make a second "instrument." In this straw, cut a finger hole about 2 inches from the non-reed end, and cut a second finger hole about 4 inches from the non-reed end. Blow the instrument first with the finger holes covered and then with each of the finger holes open. What happens to the pitch of the "note" when the finger holes are opened? Compare the note obtained with both finger holes open to that obtained from the shorter instrument from step 3. What has opening the finger holes done to the column?

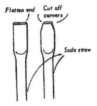

FIG. 10.2.   Alternative protocol.

ternative protocol groups discussed each step, their observations, and the explanations for their observations with their colleagues during the entire exercise. They became interested in the underlying science, and they extended the scope of their experiments more than did the cookbook protocol groups.

The cookbook group that interacted with the instructor began the exercise in the same manner as the other cookbook groups. However, after the instructor's intervention, their approach became closer to those groups who were assigned the alternative protocol.

Were both the cookbook protocol and alternative protocol groups engaged in active learning? Both groups were active. They cut straws, made "music" with their straws, and recorded data. However, only members of the alternative protocol groups were actively engaged in mentally building, testing, and refining their mental models.

So, how can we help the learner to learn in a student laboratory setting? This learning experiment, conducted in a faculty development workshop, suggests that the laboratory exercise, per se, *can* be an appropriate vehicle for reaching the desired output state. What needs changing, if the laboratory is to be successful, is the "instruction manual" for the vehicle. The instruction manual must be written in a way that encourages students to examine and test their mental models while they run the experiment. They must make predictions, but they must also compare their results to their predictions and reflect on what is happening or has happened at each step of the experiment. They must explain the bases for their predictions. They must attempt to explain discrepancies between the predictions and the actual results.

WHAT ARE THE FACTORS THAT MAKE A STUDENT LABORATORY AN ACTIVE LEARNING EXPERIENCE?

We have also examined the impact of the directions given to students on learning in a physiology laboratory in a more systematic way. The topic for the laboratory was respiratory function, and our assessment of learning was the response given by students to a question regarding the breathing pattern that occurs when conditions require an increase in the amount of fresh air reaching the alveoli (that is, increased alveolar ventilation will occur).

What happens to the breathing pattern when you exercise? The respiratory rate increases, but what happens to the depth of breathing? Does it increase, decrease, or stay the same? We have posed this question to students (Michael, 1998; Michael et al., 1999), attendees at faculty development workshops, and professional colleagues at seminars. The results are always similar. About 60% of the populations that we have polled say that the depth of breathing will either decrease or remain unchanged. When asked for the rationale for their answers, most respond that if you are breathing faster, there isn't time for you to breathe deeper. The apparent error in their mental model is that this population fails to recognize that the rate of contraction and the strength of contraction of the respiratory muscles can vary. As a result, respiratory rate and the depth of breathing can, and, in fact do, both increase to produce an increased alveolar ventilation.

How can we use a laboratory experience to help our students to build a correct mental model of this phenomenon or to correct an incorrect model? We tested about 700 undergraduate students before and after performing a laboratory activity in which they measured the effect of exercise on the rate and depth of breathing (Modell et al., 2000). The target output state for the exercise was for students to recognize that rate and depth of breathing can increase simultaneously and to correctly predict what happens to the breathing pattern when alveolar ventilation increases. To assess the input state, we tested the students prior to their running the laboratory activity. The learning experience consisted of measuring the rate and depth of breathing before and after exercising. However, three different protocols were used to direct the students.

The first protocol followed a traditional written "observe and record" (**cookbook protocol**) format. In the second treatment group, a written protocol asked students to complete a prediction table before running the experiment (**predictor protocol**). Students in the third treatment group were given the written predictor protocol but, before they performed the activity, they were also asked by one of the investigators to predict what would happen in the experiment (**instructor intervention protocol**). The instructor intervention protocol also had students show their results to the investigator so that they could compare their results to their predictions.

During the week following the laboratory, students were again tested to see if they could correctly predict the changes in ventilation that occur when an individual takes in more air. About 35% of the students with the cookbook and predictor protocols who had given incorrect answers on the pre-test were correct on the post-test. About 75% of the students who were in the group with the instructor intervention protocol were able to correct their initial error.

Because we hadn't checked to make sure that the students with the predictor protocol had actually made their predictions prior to running the activity, we assumed that the explanation for the difference between the predictor protocol and the instructor intervention was that the predictor protocol group did not follow the instructions, and, hence, behaved in a manner that was no different than the cookbook protocol group.

We repeated the experiment (Modell et al., unpublished observations), this time requiring the predictor protocol groups to show their prediction tables to the teaching assistant before carrying out the activity. The results of the follow-up experiment were essentially the same as the earlier experiment. About 30% of the students who had the cookbook and predictor protocols successfully corrected their error and about 70% of the instructor intervention protocol students successfully corrected their error.

Our interpretation of these results is that if we want to help students build and refine their mental models in the laboratory, it is not enough to have them make predictions and assume that they will actually look at the results of their experiment and compare them to their predictions. We must direct them to compare their results to their predictions and try to reconcile any differences that they might find. The cognitive science literature also supports the view that just directing students to make predictions is not sufficient (Macbeth,

2000; Smith, 1991). If they are to refine their mental models, they must compare their results to their predictions and generate explanations for their predictions and for discrepancies between their predictions and the data.

ASK, DON'T TELL

Our message is that your role in the student laboratory, in terms of helping students engage in meaningful learning, is no different from your roles in the lecture or conference room settings. First, you must establish your target output state goals. Assessing the input state is somewhat easier for the student laboratory since the activity usually follows student involvement in the lecture and conference room settings in the course. However, you must encourage students to test their own input states by directing them to make predictions about what they think will happen during the experiment and explain the bases for their predictions. You must then explicitly direct them to compare their predictions to their results to help them detect "errors" in their mental models and help them refine their mental models. Another way of expressing our message is that you must help the student recognize the elements of the scientific process and model the behavior of the successful scientist. Furthermore, this process must be made explicit for the learner.

So, how do you accomplish this? You ask students things. What do you think will happen? What do you think would have happened if we had done this instead of that? Why do you think this will happen? Why do you think that happened? How is this like what we studied last week or last semester? What are the implications of your answer if another variable changed?

You must ask these kinds of questions in the written directions that you provide for students to follow during laboratory activities. You must ask these kinds of questions when you circulate among groups of students working on a laboratory experiment. You must also ask these kinds of questions, if appropriate, when students seek clarification from you about some aspect of the laboratory. This is not an easy task. You want to help the learner to learn by giving information, but, in most cases, the learner learns when he or she is confronted with a problem that needs solving. Asking appropriate questions provides help with the process; telling answers bypasses the process.

We have examined a number of classroom settings, the kinds of activities that help promote an active learning environment in those settings, and the rationale for choosing various types of classroom activities. In the next chapter, we will explore ways in which we build learning environments in which students work together to build, test, and refine their mental models. Aspects of the techniques to be described are applicable to all classroom settings.

11

New Approaches to Science Learning: Cooperative and Collaborative Learning

CHAPTER OVERVIEW

Cooperative learning, collaborative learning, problem-based learning, and peer teaching are all approaches to learning that have become popular in recent years. They are student centered, and there is a substantial research literature demonstrating the effectiveness of these approaches to learning. Although students are "active" participants in these approaches, working in groups does not necessarily ensure that students are working within an active learning environment. Thus, the potential for these approaches may be greater than is currently being realized in many classrooms. This chapter will reexamine these approaches to learning from the perspective of creating an active learning environment in which students build and test their mental models and faculty serve as diagnosticians and facilitators.

In the three previous chapters we discussed the three traditional kinds of classroom settings that have been used in science courses—lectures, discussions, and laboratories. For each of these settings, we discussed the constraints that affect what you, the teacher, can do in that setting, and we offered some ideas for helping the learner to learn in those environments. In this chapter we will describe a number of more recently developed learning environments that are being widely discussed and implemented at all levels of education.

Learning in the classroom (and remember, not all learning occurs in the classroom) involves both teachers and students. However, there are many different ways to organize what happens in the classroom—what the teacher does and what the students do. This is another way of saying that there are many different kinds of learning experiences that teachers create. One way to characterize the differences between many of these kinds of experiences is to position them along a continuum that is said to extend from teacher-centeredness to student-centeredness.

We have been arguing that **all learning** is student-centered in the sense that it is always the learner who does the learning. Nevertheless, the ideas of teacher-centeredness and student-centeredness are useful because these terms signal important aspects of the learning environments that are being considered.

Traditional, conventional classroom teaching, regardless of the physical environment in which it occurs, is generally regarded as being **teacher-centered** because all eyes and all ears are on the teacher in the front of the class. At this end of the continuum, the operating assumption is that what the teacher does determines what the students learn and how they learn it. The focus or attention is directed primarily at the teacher. This does not mean that the students are merely passive recipients of knowledge delivered by the teacher. It does not mean that the students are not "active" some of the time. It does not mean that the students do not get a chance to talk, whether to one another or with the teacher. In a teacher-centered learning environment, learning is thought to occur as a result of what the teacher does, and the teacher becomes responsible for what is learned and what is not learned.

Student-centered approaches to learning start from a different assumption. In this view, what is learned is determined by what the students do, a view clearly in accord with our approach to helping the learner to learn. Student-centered approaches to learning do not relegate the teacher to some minor supporting role, but these approaches do define new roles for the teacher. By focusing on the learner, these approaches reinforce the idea that the teachers' job is to help the learner to learn. Perhaps most importantly, student-centered approaches to learning place the responsibility for learning where it clearly belongs, on the learner.

In recent years a number of approaches to implementing student-centered learning have been described. Although the labels that have been attached to these different schemes sound different, all of them represent variations on the theme of *students learning together*. Nevertheless, the labels have come to carry with them assumptions and implications to which practitioners often attach great importance, although others may find the distinctions drawn between approaches difficult to discern. (The difficulties encountered in reading the literature in this area range from authors making fine, nearly invisible, distinctions between seemingly similar classroom activities to authors who use three or four of the labels in the same paragraph.)

We will use the term *"group learning"* to refer to all learning environments in which students learn together.

In this chapter we will describe some examples of student-centered, group learning environments in which teachers can help the learner to learn. Our purpose is to provide background information, not to advocate one approach over another. Nor are we advocating that traditional ways of organizing classroom activities be totally abandoned in favor of the total adoption of these newer approaches. It is, however, important that you know about these approaches so that you can decide when and where incorporation of these approaches is appropriate. We will describe the following student-centered approaches to learning: collaborative learning and cooperative learning, peer teaching, case-based learning, and finally, problem-based learning.

COOPERATIVE/COLLABORATIVE LEARNING

Shafritz, Koeppe, and Soper (1988) define "cooperative learning" as "[a]n instructional method by which students cooperate in small teams to learn material that is initially presented by the teacher. The students take responsibility for their own learning, their teammates' learning and for classroom management by checking and monitoring, helping one another with problems and encouraging one another to achieve." Johnson, Johnson, and Smith (1998) state, "[c]ooperative learning is the instructional use of small groups so that students work together to maximize their own and each other's learning." Alkin (1992) offers this definition. "Cooperative learning refers to instructional methods in which students of all levels of performance work together in small groups, usually towards a group goal. *The many cooperative learning methods differ considerably from one another* (emphasis added)."

Collaborative learning is said to extend the idea of cooperative learning to creating an environment in which students, working together in groups, seek to accomplish tasks that they could not individually accomplish (Blumenfeld, Marx, Soloway, & Krajcik, 1996; Lumpe & Staver, 1995). A useful sourcebook on collaborative learning is available from the National Center for Postsecondary Teaching and Learning Assessment (Goodsell et al., 1992).

We argue that the similarities between the various ways of implementing cooperative and collaborative learning are more important than any presumed differences between them; both involve small groups of students working together to learn together.

In planning a group learning environment there are many factors that you must consider: how you will assign students to groups and for how long, the nature of the assignments you make to the groups, the distribution of tasks between group members, and how you will assess students.

You can make group assignments at random, or you can deliberately make up groups that take into account gender, ethnicity, and general performance levels of the students. In many situations (particularly if the group will work together for only a single class period or portion of a class period) it is appropriate to allow groups to form on a completely *ad hoc*, spontaneous basis. Groups may work together for only a single session or a single project, they may work together for a fixed number of weeks, or they may stay intact for the duration of the course. Decisions about how long groups will work together and how assignments to the groups will be made must be based on the context provided by your course; criteria for groups formed to meet weekly for a problem-solving session may be different from those used to establish groups that will be expected to pursue semester-long projects in and out of class.

At the college level, and particularly in the sciences, the tasks presented to groups generally involve solving problems of some sort. For example, Heller et al. (1992) and Heller and Hollabaugh (1992) describe teaching physics problem solving in cooperative groups. It is thought that there are important differences in the expected outcomes when open-ended (many possible answers, or at least no single right answer) problems are assigned rather than more limited, textbook style problems. One benefit of open-ended problems is that they generally require a greater range of knowledge and skills to solve, thereby encouraging the cooperation (or collaboration) that these educational approaches seek to foster. Problems, whatever their nature, may be small, requiring only a few minutes to solve, larger in scope, perhaps requiring a whole class session to solve, or they can be very large, requiring group effort over the entire duration of the course.

Within the group, tasks may be undifferentiated, with all students simply contributing to the group's solution of the assigned problem. However, in some implementations, tasks are explicitly assigned. For example, if the assignment to the group requires writing a report, different sections of the report are assigned to different students. If the task is to critique a scientific paper in the literature, different students can be assigned responsibility for different sections of the paper. In a problem-based learning group, one individual will be assigned the role of recorder (charged with writing out the learning issues or hypotheses generated by the group). Members of the group also divide up the list of learning issues and research each of them before the next meeting of the group. When there are different assignments or tasks in the group, these are commonly rotated between all members during the existence of the group; this is certainly the usual practice in problem-based learning groups.

In what is called the "jigsaw" approach (Aronson & Patnoe, 1997), all the students from different groups with the same assigned task first work together to develop the expertise needed and then return to work with their group to solve the problem. For example, if the problem involves the environmental consequences of the use of a particular class of pesticides, one member of the group will become the "expert" on the chemistry of these compounds, another member of the group will become the "expert" on the relevant features of the local ecology, and the third member might research the legal aspects of the situation.

Perhaps the most difficult aspect of any implementation of cooperative learning for teachers (and, not incidentally, for students) is assessment. The issue is whether you will assess individual student effort and learning or the performance (and presumably the learning) of the group as a whole. In the latter case, each individual receives the score earned by the group. It is common for teachers to employ both individual assessment and some assessment of the individual's contribution to the group's function.

PEER TEACHING

Peer tutoring has been described (Shafritz et al., 1988) as "the practice of having students of the same or similar ages assist with the instruction of other students who may need supplemental aid." The implication is that the student tutor has already learned the material while the tutee needs assistance. In this case, then, tutoring refers to the delivery of remediation. On the other hand, Alkin (1992) discusses both "reciprocal peer tutoring" and "learning-by-tutoring" teaching modalities in which both tutor and tutee are expected to learn the new material being studied. As with the other forms of group learning that we have described, there are a great many similarities and differences between the many approaches to learning called "peer teaching" (Derry, 1999).

Peer teaching can be as informal as simply asking students to solve a problem and then compare and debate answers with their nearest neighbor in the lecture hall (see chap. 8). It also includes small group problem solving (chap. 9) in the conference room. On the other hand, it can include programs in which pairs of students are instructed in some specific techniques of reciprocal teaching to be used in mastering some particular subject. For example, in a small group of students (or in dyads) each may take turns being the "teacher," asking questions to stimulate discussion, summarizing the conclusions the group reached, and perhaps asking for predictions about where the subject matter will take them next.

CASE-BASED LEARNING

The essential feature of case-based learning is that information is acquired and problem-solving skills are learned while trying to solve complex, realistic ("authentic") problems. It is important to recognize that the term "case" refers to any problem situation in whatever field of study is being pursued; in some fields or contexts this may refer to a patient problem (a "case"), but it need not refer to anything healthcare related. It is thought that the learning that ensues, by virtue of occurring within a realistic context (one within which the learner will be expected to function later), will be more readily retained and retrieved for later use (Williams, 1992).

Although it is possible to use cases in a non-group setting, most discussion of case-based learning has focused on its use in small group, cooperative, or collaborative learning.

In most implementations of case-based learning, solving the problem will require not only the application of specific course content, but will also require the students to consult other sources of information. It is also common that solving the problem will require the group to utilize the knowledge and expertise distributed among the members of the group.

Cases can be used as a means of helping students consolidate and integrate knowledge acquired from lectures and/or reading. If this is the goal, cases are usually assigned as final, culminating exercises (Michael & Rovick, 1999). On the other hand, problem-based learning (see further) uses cases as the vehicle to drive all acquisition of knowledge. The case, then, is confronted before the knowledge is acquired.

Although it is possible to organize an entire course around a series of cases with all of the learning being driven in one way or another by those cases, it is more common for cases to be used as one learning resource among many making up the course.

PROBLEM-BASED LEARNING

Problem-based learning is one form of case-based learning. However, it is an implementation that has taken on some specific, defining characteristics (Barrows, 1983; Davis & Harden, 1999). In North America, problem-based learning seems to have had its origin in medical education, specifically at McMaster University. The problem-based learning curriculum implemented at McMaster (and later at a great many other medical schools across the world) incorporated a number of specific features. Students meet periodically in small groups (typically 5 to 10 students) with a facilitator to solve a problem. Each problem takes at least two sessions to complete, with additional parts of the problem made available to the students at each session. The educational objectives pursued include learning content knowledge (the subject matter), problem-solving skills and cooperative learning skills.

When students first confront the problem, their initial task is to determine what they need to know (the "learning issues") in order to solve the problem. Between sessions each student takes responsibility for acquiring the knowledge that will be needed and brings that information back to the next session to be shared with the group. At the next session, the students' newly acquired knowledge is applied again to the first part of the problem and applied to the next part of the problem that is provided them. This continues over as many sessions as are scheduled for this particular problem. Thus, student learning is constantly driven by the requirements of solving the problem being confronted.

The roles of the facilitator in a problem-based learning session are still being debated, but it is agreed that the primary task is to help guide the group in the *process* of working together to solve the problem. That is to say, the facilitator is not viewed as a lecturer, a deliverer of information. Whether the facilitator needs to be a content expert, or should be a content expert, is unclear. In any event, it is essential that the facilitator be trained to function as a guide *not* as a lecturer.

Although problem-based learning got its start in medical schools, it has rapidly been implemented in other disciplines and at many different educational levels from K–12 (Torp & Sage, 1998) through undergraduate programs (Allen, 1997; Meirson, 1998; Rangachari, 1991), and many other professional programs (Boud & Feletti, 1997). As this diffusion has occurred, a number of different implementations have appeared, each reflecting differences in the disciplines being studied, the student populations being addressed, and a host of local factors. Although this growing diversity has provided many additional models that can be considered, it has also made it difficult to compare the success of problem-based learning as it has clearly become many possible things.

WHAT IS THE ROLE OF THE TEACHER IN A STUDENT-CENTERED CLASSROOM?

We suggested earlier in this chapter that student-centered approaches to teaching require the teacher to take on new roles in the classroom, or at least to emphasize different roles. Certainly, the teacher as deliverer of information is de-emphasized, although not necessarily eliminated, in the newer approaches we have described here. Cooper (1999) defines five roles for the teacher in a peer teaching environment, but her list applies equally well to all student-centered implementations. The teacher is, first of all, the developer of the educational program, making decisions about all of the issues just discussed. The teacher is also a model for the kinds of behaviors in which she expects her students to engage. These behaviors, the activities that the students are expected to engage in, must be coordinated, and this is another role for the teacher. The teacher must also be prepared to function as a mentor or facilitator of the students' learning efforts. Finally, the teacher has a clear role as an evaluator of student performance and learning.

DO I HAVE TO CONVERT THE WHOLE CURRICULUM?
MY WHOLE COURSE?

One obstacle preventing more teachers from trying one of the student- centered approaches just described is the belief that you must convert all aspects of your present course to the new format. A reading of the literature written by originators or early adopters of many of these approaches could certainly lead the reader to believe this position. *However, you need not throw out all of the old to be replaced by the new, and in many cases it would be inappropriate to do so.*

A more realistic scenario involves carefully and thoughtfully adding elements of, say, cooperative learning to your course and experimenting with the factors needed to make it work in your environment and with your students. As experience and confidence are gained, you can add additional elements until you have produced the course that best helps your students to learn.

However, there are at least two things to keep in mind. The introduction of group learning elements into an otherwise traditional lecture-based course will pose the problem of getting students to "play the game." You will have to explicitly assist your students in learning the new "rules," and you will have to create an environment in your classroom in which the "new" behaviors you are asking for are likely to be produced. In Chapter 7 we discussed this issue at some length.

This problem of getting the students to "play the game" is aggravated when yours is the ONLY course in which they are asked to be active learners in a group learning environment. The only possible solution to this problem is to be clear and explicit about your expectations (objectives) and to carefully build a classroom learning environment in which the students will feel safe to interact (with one another and with you) in the manner requested.

ASSESSMENT IN A GROUP LEARNING ENVIRONMENT

In any learning environment it is essential that the means of assessing student performance correspond to the course objectives. This can be particularly difficult in a group cooperative/collaborative learning environment. It is, of course, essential to determine whether students are acquiring the content that you have described as required in your objectives. In addition, if problem solving has been defined as a core objective, then this too must be assessed. Finally, in many settings, problem-based learning courses being prime examples, the behavior of students in their groups (cooperation, sharing tasks, etc.) is also viewed as being an important component of demonstrated competence; this too then must be assessed in some manner. We can not stress too strongly the importance of there being a correspondence between what you say is important and what you assess.

In Chapter 12 we will discuss approaches to student assessment that are applicable in all learning environments including ones that incorporate group learning.

GROUP LEARNING AND ACTIVE LEARNING

It should be obvious that all of the forms of group learning that have been described here require that the student be an active learner. In a group learning setting, students are interacting with one another to accomplish a common goal, the solution of a problem. All of these forms of group learning occur in a student-centered, rather than a teacher-centered, environment; learning occurs because of what the students do, not as a result of teacher delivery of information (although that may be an element in the environment).

The challenge for the instructor who wants to promote student-centered learning is to convince students who have spent most of their school life in teacher-centered environments to willingly participate in this "new" learning environment. In Chapter 7, we discussed issues and techniques related to helping students make this transition.

Part IV

Assessment in an Active
Learning Environment

Chapter

12

Assessment of Student Performance

CHAPTER OVERVIEW

A spectrum of tools is available for assessing student performance. Examples include objective exams, short answer and essay exams, portfolios, projects, practical exams, presentations, and combinations of these. Appropriate tools or combinations of tools must be used if the assessment process is to successfully provide information relevant to stated educational goals.

One of the most difficult tasks for most teachers is assessing the performance of their students, determining to what extent each individual student has attained the level of mastery defined by the course objectives. This task is a necessary one for a number of reasons: (a) students need to know whether, or to what extent, they are succeeding in mastering the material; (b) we need to certify successful completion of a body of material (our course) as a part of the students' curriculum or course of study (the biology or physics "major" or some general science requirement); and (c) in the case of students enrolled in professional programs (nursing, physical therapy, etc.), we need to certify competence to practice that profession.

It should be clearly understood that we are talking about the assessment of individual students (the assigning of grades), not the evaluation of a teaching program or some learning activity (how we, as teachers, are doing). This latter subject is dealt with in Chapter 13. Nor are we considering the issue of student achievement of standards, whether locally or nationally defined. The issue is determining how each of your students is performing relative to *your* expectations (target output states).

It has been observed that "examinations drive the curriculum." That is to say, whatever your announced educational objectives and course goals, student learning behaviors will be determined by the examinations you administer. If your goal is to establish an active learning environment in which students are expected to learn the facts *and* learn to apply them, but your exams test only the students' ability to regurgitate memorized facts, you will have made it unlikely that the students will engage in meaningful learning. Thus, the assessment tools that you employ in your course have an enormously important role in determining how and what students will learn.

The message here is a simple one, you must test what you say you value! Thus, the process of assessing student performance in your course must begin with a close look at your educational objectives (see chap. 4). What you will discover is that some objectives (knowledge of facts, being able to solve quantitative problems) are relatively easy to assess, while other objectives (being able to formulate a testable hypothesis, being able to write a scientific report) are very much harder to test.

BEFORE PROCEEDING!

List all of the forms of assessment that you have used in your teaching. Are there other approaches to assessment with which you are familiar even if you haven't personally used them in your courses? How did you decide which forms of assessment to use?

There are a large number of different forms of assessment, and there are approaches that are suitable for essentially any educational objective you want to test. Doran, Lawrenz, and Helgeson (1994) list 17 different methods and types of assessment (Table 12.1) that they classify in a variety of ways. In their book *Assessing Science Understanding*, Mintzes, Wandersee, and Novak (2000) include chapters describing nine different assessment techniques, including a number not listed by Doran (concept mapping, Vee diagrams, semantic networks, and image based). "Tests" can be made up of multiple-choice, true-false, completion, short answer, or essay items. Practical examinations are another form of "test." Other assessment tools enable you to determine student attitudes and values. In this chapter, we will discuss assessment of knowledge, application of knowledge, and practical laboratory work.

ASSESSING THE KNOWLEDGE ACQUIRED BY A STUDENT

Objective examinations (true-false, multiple-choice, completion items) are the traditional approach to asking whether students have acquired whatever

TABLE 12.1

Methods of assessment

1. True-false item	10. Inventories
2. Multiple-choice item	11. Checklist
3. Completion item	12. Peer rating
4. Short answer item	13. Self rating
5. Essay item	14. Portfolios
6. Practical examination	15. Observation
7. Papers	16. Discussion
8. Projects	17. Interview
9. Questionnaires	

Note: From Doran et al., 1994.

facts we have asked them to acquire. However, short answer and essay items, as well as papers, can also provide relatively direct insight about whether the student has a mastery of the facts. Such approaches also allow you to assess whether the student is able to use the language of the discipline in the manner defined by your objectives. You can, of course, gain similar information through discussion or interviews with the student.

ASSESSING A STUDENT'S ABILITY TO USE THE KNOWLEDGE THAT HAS BEEN ACQUIRED

The issue here is determining whether meaningful learning has occurred. Although it is common to attack objective test items (multiple choice questions) as unsuited for assessing student mastery of higher-order thinking (the ability to use information to solve problems), such an attitude is unwarranted (Sadler, 1998). You *can* write multiple choice questions that require students to apply knowledge in quite complex ways in order to select the correct answer; such questions can test the ability to solve either quantitative or qualitative reasoning problems (chap. 2). It is true, of course, that such questions are often quite difficult to write (see further).

One quite powerful approach to writing questions that determine whether students are able to solve problems with the knowledge they have acquired is to ask for qualitative predictions (increase/decrease/no change) about the response of a system. Examples of such questions from a number of different disciplines can be seen in Table 12.2.

TABLE 12.2

Examples of prediction questions from different disciplines

Based on the thermochemical data in Appendix C and LeChatelier's principle, predict whether the solubility of AgCl in H_2O increases or decreases with increasing temperature.

The acid-dissociation constant for Cu^{2+} (aq) ion is 1.0×10^{-8}. Based on this value and the acid-dissociation constant of lactic acid, predict whether a solution of copper(II) lactate will be acidic, basic or neutral.

(From Brown, LeMay, & Bursten, 2000.)

An ice-skater spins about a vertical axis through her body with her arms held out. As she draws her arms in, her angular velocity:

1. increases.
2. decreases.
3. remains the same.
4. need more information.

Compared with the applied electrical field, the electric field within a linear dialectric is
1. smaller.
2. larger
3. depends on the dialectric.

(From Mazur, 1997.)

Predict the effects (increase, decrease, no change) of the following autonomic agonists on heart rate (HR):

1. α-adrenergic
2. β-adrenergic
3. muscarinic
4. nicotinic

(From Michael & Rovick, 1999.)

More complex responses can be obtained through the use of the predictions table (Rovick & Michael, 1992; see Table 12.3 for an example). Here a large number of predictions about the response of a system are requested. Individual predictions reveal something about the students' understanding of individual relationships that underlie the function of the system, and patterns of prediction errors can tell you about the presence of important con-

TABLE 12.3
A predictions table about the control of blood pressure

Parameter	DR	RR	SS
Cardiac Contractility (CC)			
Central venous pressure (CVP)	X	X	X
Stroke volume (SV)			
Heart rate (HR)			
Cardiac output (CO)	X	X	X
Total peripheral resistance (TPR)			
Mean arterial pressure (MAP)			

DR = Direct Response before any reflex response occurs.
RR = Reflex Response to the change in MAP that occurs in DR.
SS = Steady State (new) about reflex response has occurred.
Note: From Rovick & Michael, 1992. Reprinted by permission of the American Physiological Society.

ceptual and/or reasoning difficulties (Michael, 1998; Michael et al., 1999; Michael et al., 2002) the students are having.

For example, a pattern of errors in predicting changes in CVP and CO suggests a misunderstanding of how a change in cardiac output (CO) will affect the volume of blood in the central venous compartment and hence the central venous pressure (CVP). Errors of this kind are therefore diagnostic for the possible presence of significant conceptual difficulties that the student is experiencing. A prediction table problem can be conveniently implemented using a multiple choice format (each cell in the table is a separate question with the three choices: increase, decrease, or no change). A sophisticated machine scoring system can look for patterns of answers in such a set of questions, or you can carry out such an analysis using visual inspection.

One approach to using multiple choice questions to assess meaningful learning is the use of follow-up questions requesting the student to provide an explanation for the answer he or she chose for the preceding question. Table 12.4 illustrates one way this might be done. Here, the student is asked to write a brief explanation for the answer to question 2. Such explanations, even when offered for correct answers, can be quite diagnostic about the level and extent of the student's understanding of the phenomena about which questions are being asked. This approach does require, of course, that you read and grade the explanations offered, a potentially time-consuming task. However, you needn't ask for explanations for every multiple choice answer in your exam. One way to sample explanations for a large number of

TABLE 12.4

Justifying an answer to a multiple choice question

A container is divided by a membrane into two compartments in which ions can be placed. One compartment is labeled "inside" and the other is labeled "outside." The membrane is permeable to both cation A^+ and B^+. It is not permeable to other cations that are distributed equally between the compartments. The equilibrium potential of cation A^+ is +50 mv. The equilibrium potential for cation B^+ is –50 mv.

1. When the equilibrium potential for cation B+ is measured, the concentration of B+ is
    A. greater in the "inside" chamber.
    B. greater in the "outside" chamber.
    C. the same in both chambers.

2. If the conductance of the membrane to A^+ is less than the conductance of the membrane to B^+, the resting potential of the system
    A. will be between –50 mv and 0 mv.
    B. will be 0 mv.
    C. will be between 0 mv and +50 mv.
    D. can't be determined without more information.

    Briefly justify your answer.

3. In this experiment, the concentration gradient for cation A^+ is
    A. greater than the concentration gradient for cation B^+.
    B. equal to the concentration gradient for cation B^+.
    C. less than the concentration gradient for cation B^+.

different questions is to prepare multiple versions of your exam in which explanations are requested for different questions in each version.

There is another approach to requiring students to explain their answer to a multiple choice question. Each answer in the "stem" question can direct the student to a follow-up multiple choice question that requests an explanation for the answer to the stem question. Table 12.5 illustrates one such question and its follow-up questions. The choices that are presented can be generated from student responses in class and in any written work. Thus, the explanations chosen by the students is diagnostic for common student conceptual difficulties (Michael et al., 2002).

Assessment formats that require the students to generate a "free response" (short answer or essay exams, papers) provide an opportunity for

TABLE 12.5

Obtaining explanations for an answer to a multiple choice question using follow-up multiple choice questions

An individual plays a vigorous set of tennis. He notices that his heart is beating quite rapidly.

3. While playing tennis, the strength of his heart beat will
    a) increase
    b) decrease
    c) remain unchanged

3A. The strength of his heart beat will *increase* because:
    a) the increase of heart rate directly causes an increase in the strength of contraction of the heart
    b) of a response that increases the rate at which blood is pumped out of the heart
    c) the tissues of the body need more blood flow

3B. The strength of his heart beat will *decrease* because:
    a)
.   b)
    c)

3C. The strength of his heart beat will remain *unchanged* because:
    a)
    b)
    c)

Note: From Michael, 1998. Reprinted by permission of the American Physiological Society.

determining what the student knows and how well he or she is able to use that knowledge. Such assessment tools also represent the most direct approach to determining how well the student can use the language of the discipline. However, the time required to grade essays or papers can be prohibitively high if you have a large number of students and/or must do the grading yourself. There is also the inherent problem of maintaining consistency in your grading from student to student. One useful approach to accomplishing this is to write a "correct answer" to the question and preassign point values for each of the features of this answer. You can then use the model answer as a template against which to judge each student's answer.

If your intention is to determine whether meaningful learning has occurred, you will want to see if the students can solve problems involving novel situations that they have not previously seen. In science classes this is usually quite easy to do because questions about the same concept or principle can always be imbedded in a seemingly different situation or system (the problems look different on the surface but are identical at a deeper level).

If you have as one of the objectives of your course that students will learn to solve certain types of problems, or use certain problem-solving strategies, you may want to devise assessment tools that do that independently of whether the students have learned the course content or have actually generated a correct answer. For example, in problem-based learning courses (see chap. 11) in which particular emphasis is placed on learning to use hypothetico-deductive reasoning to solve problems, examinations have been developed that assess the student's ability to apply each of the required steps in the process. Even if the student was unsuccessful in reaching a correct solution to the problem, he or she may display a competence for carrying out each step in the process.

ASSESSING GROUP WORK

When students are learning in a cooperative learning environment (see chap. 11) you may want to assess their participation or contribution to the group process. This can be done in a variety of ways. Checklists can be used to describe the behaviors you wish to assess with students assessing themselves and each other. If there is a group facilitator or tutor, that individual can also rate each individual member of the group and the group as a whole. You must recognize that students will need help learning to carry out such evaluations. Delivering useful feedback is a task that is difficult for most of us.

ASSESSING A STUDENT'S ABILITY TO CARRY OUT WORK IN THE LABORATORY

If you need to assess your students' work in the laboratory, and if the issue is whether they can *perform* certain procedures correctly, the best approach is to observe their performance in the laboratory. This should be done in a systematic way using a checklist, a detailed description of each of the important steps in the procedure, and how well the student carried out that particular step.

Written exams can be used to assess a student's ability to design an experiment, analyze experimental data, or determine if data supports a hypothesis. Another approach is to have students assemble a portfolio that contains their work from the laboratory over the academic term. This has the advantage of documenting the progress that each student has made and makes it possible to identify specific components of the students' lab skills that need improvement.

USE OF PROBLEMS, CASES, AND SCENARIOS
TO PROVIDE THE "CONTEXT" FOR ASSESSMENT

One of the hallmarks of meaningful learning (chap. 2) is the ability to apply the knowledge that has been acquired to a novel situation, one that has not previously been encountered. Problems or cases can provide a novel context in which students can be asked to demonstrate their mastery of your educational objectives. They can be brief, two or three sentences, descriptions of a situation, longer stories about a patient or a problem, or extended (many pages) descriptions of some evolving issue.

Any of the assessment instruments that we have discussed can be used in the context of a problem or case: short answer, essays, concept maps, even multiple choice questions can be used to evaluate the state of students' understanding. Furthermore, you can ask students to demonstrate their analytical skills as well as their understanding. Questions such as "how would you determine ...?," "what would you do next ...?" "what data would you need to acquire in order to ...?" can enable you to evaluate not only what the students know but also how they think.

WHAT ARE THE COSTS AND BENEFITS
OF DIFFERENT FORMS OF ASSESSMENT?

As we mentioned at the outset, student assessment is always a difficult task, one that is made more difficult as the number of students to be assessed increases. However important this task is, you cannot spend all your time assessing students; there are many other tasks that you must accomplish. That being the case, it is important that the assessment tools that you choose are able to measure what you want measured at a "cost" that is acceptable.

In general, the "cost" of most concern to you is the time that must be spent generating the assessment instrument and then scoring the "test" once it is administered. There are a number of ways that you can minimize the time required to generate an assessment instrument. Building a bank of questions from which to select the items to be included on any particular exam eventually yields considerable savings. It also has the virtue of, over time, providing information about the degree of difficulty of the items in your question bank.

Scoring objective exam items, of course, can be done by machines, and this can have the added benefit of providing statistical information about student performance on your examination. In some circumstances students can score their own exams or those of other members of the class. Finally, in many situations teaching assistants can be used to grade exams.

Computer technology can help with the problems of grading time and consistency. For example, we recently began administering exams with short answer questions over the Internet. Students log onto a website to take the exam. This data is then inserted into a spreadsheet. The instructor can see each student's answer to a specific question in turn without having to spend time deciphering handwriting and turning exam pages. This format also allows the instructor to easily review answers that have already been graded should a question of consistency arise.

Formal student assessments may provide much of the evidence you use to assign a grade to each student. However, the results of assessments also provide you with valuable information about the students' output state as well as providing evidence about how successful your active learning environment is in helping the learner to learn. We will consider this issue further in Chapter 13.

Chapter

13

How Do I Know It's Working?

CHAPTER OVERVIEW

It is essential to determine whether the new approach you have adopted is, in fact, helping your students in the classroom. You will want to assess how well it is working on a day-to-day basis, determining if your students are engaged in more meaningful learning and how your students are responding to this new learning environment.

Let us assume that you have decided that the helping the learner to learn mindset may have some benefit in your classroom, and you are willing to give it a try. To convince yourself that it will make a difference for you and your students, you want some evidence in your own classroom that students are engaging in more meaningful learning. So, the question is, "How do I evaluate this approach? How do I know it's working?"

BEFORE PROCEEDING!

What are you currently doing to determine if you are successful in the classroom? What would you do to determine if a more student-centered, active learning environment is "working?"

There are three different questions that we need to consider. First, how do I know it's working on a day-to-day basis in the classroom? Second, how can I determine whether the process has benefitted my students? Finally, how can I document the response of my students to the learning environment that I have created in my classroom? The first question deals with classroom assessment, the second with designing appropriate testing instruments, and the third with course evaluation.

Any attempt to determine if helping the learner to learn "works" presupposes that you have, in fact, made changes in your course. Have you explicitly included course objectives that require students to achieve a level of meaningful learning, not just memorization of facts? Have you attempted to implement learning environments that will assist students in achieving the goals that you have set for them? Are you holding them accountable for achieving these goals, assessing their level of performance in ways that are appropriate? If the answer to each of these questions is "yes," you can now turn to how to determine if you are being successful.

HOW DO I KNOW IT'S WORKING
ON A DAY-TO-DAY BASIS IN MY CLASSROOM?

In Chapter 5 we discussed the role of the teacher as a diagnostician, continuously assessing the state of her or his students. The key to making such assessments is interacting with your students in every learning environment that you have created. With such feedback, it is not difficult to assess the extent to which students are reaching the target output state goals you have established.

The classroom assessment techniques described by Angelo (1993) and Angelo and Cross (1993) can also be used to obtain valuable feedback. Many of the examples they describe rely on anonymous, written responses by students to a particular question or set of questions. The process takes little class time and, because of the nature of the questions asked or the designs of the surveys to be completed, takes minimal time outside of class to read the students' responses.

You can obtain information about the class as a whole by soliciting public responses from small discussion groups, obtaining anonymous responses from all members of the class, or requesting predictions about the results of perturbing a system by a show of hands.

However, you may be interested in learning how well your new approach to teaching is working for each individual student. One easy way to monitor each student's progress is to have each student periodically turn in an index card with the student's name, the date, and either a question that is puzzling him or a comment regarding the student's perception of her progress in the course. This can be done on a daily or on a weekly basis. By having each student report on his or her progress, each card becomes an entry in a "learning journal" with which you can monitor each student's progress from his or her perspective. In addition, it provides a source of feedback about where misunderstandings arise in the class and the prevalence of any confusing points or misunderstandings. It also provides another indication of the input state and provides a source of questions that can be answered in class to better help the learner to learn.

HOW CAN I DOCUMENT THAT THE PROCESS HAS HELPED MY STUDENTS?

If the process has helped our students engage in meaningful learning, they should perform better on course exams that test for meaningful learning. Although this statement may seem obvious, it is critical to recognize that our exams must test if our students have achieved what you have defined as your target output state objectives. If the output goals are to be able *to do* A, B, and C, the exams that you administer must test the student's *ability to do* A, B, and C. The target output goals must be reflected by the exam. So, how do you design exams to test what you want tested, and how do you design those exams so that they can be graded in a reasonable amount of time?

In Chapter 12 we discussed a wide variety of approaches to assessing student performance. These can be categorized as assessments that can be objectively scored (whether or not a machine is used), those that result in the student writing something, and those in which the student's performance of some task is evaluated. The key to successfully assessing meaningful learning, however, lies not in the nature of the assessment but in the nature of the task set for the student.

If all we ask of students is that they recall memorized information, we will have no idea whether they "understand" that material, or whether they can use it in some way to accomplish something (beyond recall of the information itself). We will not know if meaningful learning has occurred. On the other hand, if we give students a problem to solve, particularly if it is one that they have not previously seen, we cannot only determine if they have a command of the facts (whether they can recall them) but also if they can manipulate those facts, do something with them, to reach the goal of solving a problem.

Finally, we can obtain information about the progress of the class as a whole by using a pre-test/post-test assessment design (Modell, 1992; Wu, Krajcik, & Soloway, 2001). This technique samples the input state of the class with respect to specific concepts that are part of the target output state objectives. For example, on the first day of class, each student is given 1 to 3 pre-test questions that address a sampling of the key concepts in "non-technical" language. Students are told not to identify themselves on the paper and that their responses will not affect their grade or any other decisions related to the course. By having 10 to 15 students answer the same questions, representative answers to 20 to 30 question related to the key concepts in the course can be obtained from a class of 150 students. The exercise requires only 5 to 10 minutes of class time. By testing these same concepts in language related to the course on the final exam, group data can be obtain with which to compare group performance on the pre-test questions. If, for example, 15% of those tested provided correct answers on the pre-test, and 85% of the class provided correct responses on the final exam, one would conclude that the learning environment helped the students to build appropriate mental models related to the application of the concept. If, however, 40% answered correctly on the pre-test, and 40% answered correctly on the final exam, we could conclude that the course did not help students build appropriate mental models of the target concept.

HOW CAN I DOCUMENT MY STUDENTS' RESPONSES TO THE LEARNING ENVIRONMENT?

Many faculty who attend our workshops express a concern about student course evaluation forms typically completed near the end of the course. These instructors note that adopting the helping the learner to learn mindset will create a learning environment in which students will actually be required to think instead of memorizing a body of information. Their concern is that, because students are not used to engaging in meaningful learning, they will return negative course evaluations, and, as a result, the administration will discourage classroom reform. We should, therefore, discuss the course evaluation process that exists at many institutions and examine ways that such evaluations can be designed to provide more useful information about the course being evaluated.

The course evaluation forms currently used in many institutions are based on a number of underlying assumptions, that are most valid in a very teacher-centered learning environment.

1. Response items focus on the instructor and the way the instructor presents information (e.g., speaking style, use of audio-visual aids, manner in which instructor conveyed information, etc.). This, of course, assumes that the learning environment is a passive one in which the predominant activity is a lecture by the instructor.
2. It is assumed that the degree of learning that occurs depends on the instructor, not on the student. Response items focus primarily on the instructor's performance in the class, not the students' performance in the class.

3. Students are assumed to have the expertise to determine what are, and what are not, appropriate learning objectives for this course. Response items ask students to rate the course in terms of appropriateness of learning objectives.

4. Students are assumed to have the expertise to evaluate the quality of the learning resources used in the class, and it is assumed that they are familiar with all of the learning resources that are available to the instructor for potential use in the class. Response items ask students to rate the textbook and other written materials used in the class. This implies that "ideal" resources are available, and the question asks whether the instructor has used these "ideal" resources.

5. It is assumed that students have the expertise to evaluate use of class time. Response items focus on various aspects of class time management. For example, a common item on course evaluation forms asks students whether class time was used effectively. Without knowing the instructional goals for each class, students cannot make a determination about how effectively class time was used. Most students, because of prior educational background, would say that an instructor who delivers a lot of information to them in a short period of time (e.g., tells them what they "need to know" to pass the exam) uses class time effectively. However, if the goal of the class period is to have students learn to solve problems by engaging in problem-solving activities, telling them the "answers" without having them engage in the process is not effective use of time.

The validity of each of these assumptions is certainly open to question. Some are definitely not valid when an active learning environment is being evaluated. Hence, the result of most current course evaluation surveys is a reflection of "customer satisfaction" that does not provide an accurate reflection of the effectiveness of the learning environment.

An appropriate course evaluation survey however, can provide valuable information regarding the learning environment. The first step in designing such a survey is to ask, "What information should be sought on the survey?" Just as in other activities, we define a set of target output goals for the learning environment. Reaching some of these goals depends on the actions of the instructor. Others depend on the actions of the students. Still others may depend on how well the physical environment and the resources that are used in the class contribute to the success of the learning environment. If we want to assess the learning environment, we should seek data that will allow evaluation of all elements of the learning environment. In the type of learning environment that we have been discussing in this book, the learning that takes place depends on three essential factors, (a) the effectiveness of the instructor in helping the learner to learn; (b) the actions of the students as responsible learners; and (c) the resources available to support the learning environment.

In an active learning environment, the primary role of the instructor is not to disseminate information. It is to facilitate learning. Hence, survey items should be directed toward learning how well the instructor performed this role. Did the instructor create a safe learning environment? How well did the instructor communicate with the class? How available was the instructor for answering questions? Other examples of items directed toward assessing the instructor's role are shown in Table 13.1.

In the helping the learner to learn model, it is essential that students take responsibility for their own learning. Hence, if a meaningful evaluation of the learning environment is to be achieved, the importance of the students' role must be acknowledged, and information regarding student behavior must be

TABLE 13.1
Sample items related to evaluation of the instructor

The statements are intended to be presented in a format that requests the students to respond on a 5-point Likert scale ranging form strongly disagree to strongly agree.

- The course goals and expectations of me were made clear by the instructor.
- The instructor was well-prepared for class.
- The instructor's presentations and explanations were clear.
- The instructor answered students' questions to the best of his/her ability.
- The instructor developed a feeling of mutual goodwill conducive to learning.
- The instructor listened carefully to me and other students.
- The instructor gave helpful oral or written feedback on student performance (tests, projects, etc.).
- The instructor sought and was responsive to student feedback concerning assignments or other aspects of the course.
- The quizzes and exams were consistent with the stated learning objectives.
- The instructor was readily available for assistance outside of class, if needed.
- The instructor was concerned whether or not students learned the material.
- The instructor demonstrated sensitivity to students' differences and their needs.
- The instructor modeled the problem-solving process that he/she expected me to learn.
- The exams tested my ability to integrate and use the information that was covered in class assignments.
- The instructor helped me understand errors that I made on exams.
- The assignment to (specify assignment) was a valuable learning experience.

obtained. Students must be asked to reflect on their own behavior. Did they come to class prepared? Did they ask questions when things did not make sense? Did they use the course objectives as a study guide? Other examples of items directed toward assessing the students' role are shown in Table 13.2. Finally, data must be obtained regarding the resources available for the course. These resources include the textbook and other resource material, but they also include the physical environment in which the class was held. Were the physical attributes of the room (e.g., temperature, background noise level) conducive to learning? During discussions, could you hear the comments of

TABLE 13.2
Sample items related to evaluation of the students

Most of the statements are intended to be presented in a format that requests the students to respond on a 5-point Likert scale ranging form strongly disagree to strongly agree. Others have the five potential responses listed with the item.

- I came to class prepared for the day's discussion.
- I felt comfortable voicing my confusion in class.
- I asked questions when I did not follow the discussion.
- I reviewed the material covered in class. (Never, Only before quizzes/exams, Once a week, Several times a week, After each class)
- I contributed to my group's discussions during group work.
- I felt that the learning environment was a safe environment in which I could raise any issue that concerned me.
- I sought help from the instructor when I was having trouble with the material. (Never, Occasionally, Usually, Most of the time, Always)
- I offered constructive criticism and suggestions for improving the learning environment when I felt as if the learning environment was not "working" for me.
- I reviewed quizzes/exams to discover where I had made errors when taking the quiz/exam. (Never, Occasionally, Usually, Most of the time, Always)
- I was in the classroom ready to begin the day's work when the class period was scheduled to begin. (Never, Occasionally, Usually, Most of the time, Always)
- I accepted responsibility for my learning.
- I used the course learning objectives to guide my studying.
- I drew pictures to help me understand and answer questions on exams. (Never, Occasionally, Usually, Most of the time, Always)
- I used some of the study techniques that I learned in this class for other courses.
- When we did group work, I tried to help my group members understand the mechanisms that we were discussing.

colleagues? Other examples of items directed toward assessing the contribution of the resources used in the class are shown in Table 13.3.

Our discussion has focused on items included in the course evaluation survey that are generally presented in the form of a statement to which students respond on a 5-point Likert scale ranging from strongly disagree to strongly agree. Many course evaluations also provide space for the student to respond to two general questions: (1) What did you like about this course? and (2) What, if anything, did you dislike about this course? The responses to these questions seldom provide meaningful data to the instructor (or to the administration) because (1) "liking or disliking" may have little to do with the learning that took place, and (2) the responses are often reported as a list of comments that are not associated with the other individual comments of the respondent. For example, a very positive comment about some feature of the course made by a student who liked everything about the course carries a different weight than a similar comment about that feature of the course from a student who was critical of everything else in the course. In most course evaluations, this distinction is lost.

There are, however, two brief questions that can be asked in a short free-form manner that do provide valuable feedback for improving the course and for conveying information about the course to the administration. The questions are (1) What one thing can the instructor do to make this

TABLE 13.3

Sample items related to evaluation of the resources for the course

The statements are intended to be presented in a format that requests the students to respond on a 5-point Likert scale ranging form strongly disagree to strongly agree.

- I used a book or books other than the assigned text for my primary source of written information in this class.
- I found the class handouts useful as study aids.
- I found the computer programs that we used in class helpful learning aids.
- I went to the computer lab during open lab hours to work on the computer programs.
- I went to the computer lab during open lab hours to ask the T.A.s for help.
- The T.A.s in the computer lab were a valuable resource.
- The visual aids and computer programs that were used in class discussions helped clarify concepts for me.
- I used the computer programs that were available to me for use at home as study aids.
- During class, I could hear what classmates were saying and asking most of the time.
- The physical environment of the classroom was conducive to learning.

class a better learning environment? and (2) What one thing can you, as a student, do to make this class a better learning environment? These questions reinforce the reality that the success of a course is dependent as much on the student taking responsibility for his or her learning as it is on what the instructor does in the course. These questions encourage the student to reflect on the learning experiences encountered while taking the course and place an emphasis on improving the learning environment rather than declaring likes and dislikes about the instructor.

There is one more type of question that can be included in the course evaluation form that gives an indication of "how well it went." The responses to this question can potentially be used in the next offering of the course to help orient students to the learning environment. Of course, as is true with any request for feedback from students, you must be careful what you wish for and be prepared to look honestly and objectively at the responses. The question is, "What one thing would you tell students in the next offering of this course that, in retrospect, you would have liked someone to tell you about this course to make it a more rewarding experience?" The answers to this question can form the basis of an additional discussion of expectations for the class that complements the activities that we included in our discussion of preparing the students to participate in an active learning environment (chap. 7).

So, how do I know it's working? I have to interact with students on a daily basis; I have to keep my target output state goals in mind when I prepare course examinations; when I design course evaluation forms, I have to address the target output state goals for the environment and recognize that the students contribute as much to success of a course as does the instructor when I design course evaluation forms. The information gained from all three of these approaches to assess how well things are "working" is exactly the kind of information that we need to consider if we want to improve our ability to help the learner to learn. We must take this information, and ask ourselves why did something work and why did something else not work? We must become reflective practitioners. We will discuss what it means to be a reflective practitioner in the next chapter.

IS IT WORKING BETTER THAN MY OLD APPROACH?

It is inevitable that this question will occur to you. However, in a very real sense the question is unanswerable because your goals for your students are now quite different than they were before the change. If you believe that your new goals are appropriate for your course and your students, and if your students are reaching these goals, then you can conclude that you are being successful.

Chapter

14

The Teacher
as a Reflective Practitioner

CHAPTER OVERVIEW

A defining characteristic of professionals is their ability to reflect on what they are doing and what happens as a consequence. The scientist in the laboratory is a reflective practitioner. The teacher, whose job it is to help the learner to learn, must also be a reflective practitioner.

TEACHING AND "DOING" SCIENCE

When you go into the laboratory to "do" science, you behave in a certain way. You start with some question about nature ... what is the relationship between X and Y, why do all Z's have A's, etc. Based on your knowledge of the field and your reading of the current literature, you formulate a hypothesis that represents an answer to your question. Next, you devise an experiment to test your hypothesis. You prepare to do the experiment by designing an appropriate experimental protocol, and then you assemble or build the equipment that your experiment calls for. The techniques you decide to employ are most often based on the techniques that others have used in the research they have published. That done, you can actually do the experiment, repeating it as many times as is needed to gather all of the data you need. Finally, you analyze the data and decide if the results you obtained confirm your hypothesis. Then you start over again.

In reality, things rarely go so smoothly. Problems abound when one attempts to do research. Techniques you planned to use don't seem to work as they did in your previous experiment or in a colleague's published research. Sometimes what worked on Monday doesn't seem to work on Tuesday. The protocol you devised turns out to be unworkable for reasons that are initially unclear. What do you do to overcome these problems?

You start, of course, by paying attention *to everything* that happens in your lab, because you first have to recognize that a problem is present before you can solve it. You also think about, reflect on, *everything* you do. You go back to the literature, and you confer with your colleagues doing similar work. You ask questions about the problems, and you formulate hypotheses to explain them. You then attempt to test these hypotheses by changing what you do in the lab. Doing science is a process that involves repeated hypothesis formulating and testing.

BEFORE PROCEEDING!

In what ways does the process we have just described for "doing" science relate to what you do, or should do, in teaching (science)?

THE REFLECTIVE PRACTITIONER

Donald Schön (1983), in his seminal book *The Reflective Practitioner: How Professionals Think in Action*, describes what it is that practitioners of a number of different professions do as they practice their profession. Although the examples of professions that he studied (architecture, psychotherapy, town planning, management) seem far removed from teaching, his descriptions of how these professionals behave are very much applicable to practitioners of the teaching profession.

Schön begins by observing that much of what a professional does is based on what he calls "knowing-in-action" or "knowing-in-practice," that fund of knowledge that the professional develops from repeated interaction with essentially similar cases or problems. This knowledge is seemingly automatic and almost always tacit; practitioners find it extremely difficult to articulate why they did what they did and how they did it.

However, when the situation confronted by professionals differs in significant ways from the usual, or when the results of the usual actions are different than expected (if something "surprising" occurs), they need to "reflect" on what has happened. They need to think about what they did and why. They need to think about how their present situation may differ from all those past situations in which they developed the "knowledge-in-action." This process of "reflection-in-action" makes it possible for them to alter what they do in order to achieve the outcomes desired for the current problem.

Schön goes on to observe that "when someone reflects-in-action, he becomes a researcher in the practice context." Hypotheses are generated in an attempt to gain some understanding of what it was about the current situation that led to the surprising (usually, undesired) outcome. Was this problem different than previous problems? If so, in what ways? Was there something about the actions taken now that resulted in the undesirable outcome? Once such questions are formulated, an experiment can be carried out. If I change this factor will the outcome improve, will it be closer to the desired outcome? If the current problem is really characterized by *this* not *that*, are there other actions that will lead to a desired outcome?

Sometimes this "reflection-in-action" takes place after the fact, when the problem has been solved or the issue being dealt with has been resolved. The purpose, then, is to figure out what should be done next time a similar problem is encountered. However, often "reflection-in-action" takes place while the professional is in the midst of the interaction with the situation or problem. This can be much more difficult since the practitioner is both doing something and thinking about what he or she is doing. Furthermore, whatever she is doing is changing the situation while she is doing it! The ability to carry out "reflection-in-action" is one major component of what makes a professional a professional because it provides the capability of applying what one knows to deal with new and novel problems.

THE SCIENCE TEACHER AS REFLECTIVE PRACTITIONER

It should be clear that the scientist in the laboratory is a "reflective practitioner" in the sense that Schön uses that term, even if the researcher has never heard of this term. Successful research requires a constant reflection of everything that is occurring in the lab, even those things that have been successfully employed in past experiments. Every day, the researcher must ask him or herself, what worked yesterday? What do I have to change today to help my research progress in the way I want it to? It would appear that part of being a successful researcher, most often a tacit aspect of it, is the ability to think about what you are doing.

It should be equally obvious that the teacher in the classroom must also be a reflective practitioner (Zeichner & Liston, 1996). Planning every instructional intervention is a kind of experiment. If my students are starting at A and I want them to get to B, then I will have them do X and Y. You assess the students' output state after engaging in your planned educational activities to determine if the activities were successful ... did the students get to B? If not, what went wrong? Was your definition of the desired output state B too vague? Or was it, perhaps, too advanced for your students? Was your assessment of their input state accurate? Perhaps they didn't know as much as you thought they did. In Chapter 5 we discussed the teacher's role as a diagnostician. To succeed as a diagnostician, one must be reflective.

Sometimes that reflection occurs before the fact, as one is planning to do something (anything) in the classroom. Other times the reflection is after the fact, when you ask how yesterday's lab went (did the students reach the output state you had intended) or whether last semester's course achieved all that you had expected. Sometimes the reflection takes place while you are in the midst of an interaction with your class. Did that student understand the answer I gave to her question? What does the class's answer to my last prediction question tell me about their present state of understanding? That group in the corner is struggling to solve the current problem. What's the source of their difficulty?

The message here is that if your job is to help the learner to learn and you want to improve this process, you must treat this activity in the same way as you would treat any other research endeavor. Unlike the task of merely delivering information, helping the learner to learn is a research endeavor. Each encounter with students raises new questions about how they learn and what kind of help they need to learn. As with other research endeavors, progress depends on learning more about the elements in the process, and this can only be done by testing our own mental models of the situation (e.g., generating and testing hypotheses). Thus, to continue to grow in one's ability to help the learner to learn, one must be a reflective practitioner. This practice also impacts the issue of teaching as a scholarly effort, a topic that we will discuss in Chapter 16.

Part V

Summing Up

15

The Challenges of Helping
the Learner to Learn

CHAPTER OVERVIEW

Teachers considering adopting the helping the learner to learn mindset cite several challenges that they see as standing in their way of doing so: "covering" all the material in their course, having to abandon all their old teaching materials, the resistance of students to this approach to teaching, concerns about negative course evaluations, criticism from their colleagues, and fears of losing control of their classroom. Although these are all valid issues to be confronted, in many cases the real problem is the instructors' conviction that their job is to tell students things.

If you are like many of the instructors that we and others who run faculty development workshops encounter in active learning workshops, you have reached the point where you are thinking, "Creating an active learning environment and helping the learner to learn sounds good, but I would have trouble doing this in my classroom because.... "

BEFORE PROCEEDING!

What are the challenges that face you as you consider implementing a "helping the learner to learn" approach to your own teaching?

It is interesting that when we ask faculty what challenges they face in instituting active learning in their classrooms, several broad issues generally surface. Let's examine each of these to see if, indeed, they are real impediments to implementing the helping the learner to learn mindset.

HOW WILL I COVER ALL OF THE NECESSARY CONTENT?

The most prevalent challenge cited is, "If I take time to let students engage in group discussion or other forms of active learning, I won't have time to cover all of the content that I have to cover." This statement usually reflects two concerns. First, the content that the instructor decides the student should be exposed to requires more time than may be available. The second concern is articulation within the curriculum. "If I don't cover everything, students will not be prepared for courses later in the curriculum for which my course is a prerequisite." Also implicit in this challenge are the assumptions that (a) "If I don't say it in class, students won't 'get it'"; and (b) "Students will 'get it' if I tell them about it in class." Practical experience, however, confirms that both of these assumptions are false. Regardless of the number of times they are told, students will "get it" only when they are ready to "get it" and not before. How many times have you repeated something in class only to find out that the majority of the class couldn't correctly answer the questions covering that material on the exam?

As we have discussed, our goal is to help students engage in meaningful learning. We help them assemble a set of facts, but we are equally concerned about students learning how to use those facts (e.g., in problem solving). If students are not able to put those facts into an appropriate framework (i.e., a mental model), meaningful learning has not occurred, and the factual database is of little utility. However, if students build an appropriate framework, they are better able to make sense of new facts as they encounter them. These new facts may be encountered in class, in the assigned text, or when studying related material. Hence, we argue that it may not be necessary to use class time to cover *all* of the content that many instructors deem "necessary." If the student has access to an appropriate textbook, if it covers all of the content deemed necessary for the course, the course content has been "delivered." If there is concern that *all* of the content must be addressed in the course, reading assignments covering content not specifically dealt with in class can be made and included as testable material (that is, listed as output goals).

Our discussion thus far has assumed that the time required for active learning activities precludes including all of the intended content in the allotted class time. However, creating an active learning environment focused on meaningful learning may actually provide an opportunity to cover *more* content rather than less. In a passive learning environment, content is delivered to the students without considering their input state as the course progresses. Hence time may be spent delivering content that the students have already acquired. In addition, some of the content you want to present may require only a simple extension of the mental models that the students are building. In this case, you may be spending time stating the obvious. Helping the learner build and test appropriate mental models, however, may allow students to consider the material in more depth. This is illustrated by the following comments made by Allen Emerson (in Bosworth & Hamilton, 1994), a math instructor, in a monograph dealing with collaborative learning (one method of promoting active learning through group work; see chap. 11).

> When I began to work with groups, I was a traditional mathematics teacher. I lectured, and students listened. I began to change not because I had read the studies on collaborative learning but because I was frustrated. I never found time to lecture on all the material that students needed for subsequent courses without overrunning their understanding. Moreover, after almost twenty years, I had exhausted every trick that I knew to overcome students' hatred of mathematics and their resentment at having to take a noncredit course that does not figure in the calculation of their grade point average. Students refused to engage mathematical problems, nor were they capable of conceptualizing or articulating mathematical ideas. Teaching collaboratively has enabled me to get through more material, and students have achieved a deeper understanding, worked harder, and enjoyed it. (p. 83)

IF I ADOPT THE HELPING THE LEARNER TO LEARN MINDSET, I HAVE TO DISCARD THE PASSIVE LEARNING ENVIRONMENT RESOURCES THAT I HAVE DEVELOPED OVER THE YEARS AND START OVER

The idea that an active learning environment requires visual aids, problems, and other resources that are completely different from those used in a passive learning environment is erroneous. As we discussed when we examined the learning experience in Chapter 6, the question is not so much what resources should I use, but how should I use the resources that I have? The same data plots, figures, and other resources are valuable in both environments. In a passive learning environment, the instructor tells the students what the visual says. In an active learning environment, the instructor asks the students what the visual tells them.

Just as it is true that it takes longer to prepare a new lecture or laboratory exercise than to revise an existing lecture or rewrite a protocol for a student laboratory, the time required for designing new active learning activities is greater than the preparation time for revising established active learning activities.

Another assumption implied by this challenge is that the transition between passive and active learning environments must be all-or-none. This assumption is also false. For most people, the transition is gradual. When a colleague decided that she wanted to create an active learning environment in her classroom, she decided that in the first week, she would ask the students one question. In the next week, she would ask two questions, and, as she gained more experience, she would add more active learning activities. She was surprised to find, however, that, after asking questions for the students to discuss on the first day, the response of the students to this kind of activity was so enthusiastic that she felt it necessary to accelerate her implementation timetable. In a very short time, her rule of thumb for classroom activities became "ask, don't tell."

STUDENTS RESIST NON-LECTURE ENVIRONMENTS

Many instructors claim that the reason that they can't try an active learning approach is that their students won't stand for it. This is true if the students believe that the "rules of the game" are that the instructor will tell us what we need to know to pass the exam.

As we discussed in Chapter 7, students will play the game that leads to success in the class as long as the rules of the game are explicitly defined, and the instructor follows the same rules. Hence, this challenge is really not an impediment as long as the instructor makes the expectations for the course clear to the students and creates a safe learning environment in which the students feel comfortable taking intellectual risks.

The importance of a safe learning environment cannot be emphasized too much when one is considering how to involve students in an active learning environment. There are several "tricks" that can be used to ease students into embracing this type of learning environment. First, if students feel as if the instructor cares about their learning, and they recognize that they are not anonymous occupants of chairs in the room, they will be more willing to participate. We recommend that instructors learn and use their students' names. It may not be reasonable to learn all of the students' names, but using names in class certainly sends the message to the class that the instructor has taken the time to become acquainted with students and that they, in fact, are accountable and are expected to participate in class discussions.

Another "trick" is to ease the class into the active learning environment. On the first day of class, ask one question for them to answer. On the second day of class, ask two questions. By moving gradually from a passive to active learning environment, students begin to recognize (1) that they already know something about the course content, (2) that they are learning more, (3) that the time period spent in class seems to be shorter than in the passive learning environment. As a result, they not only "buy into the game," they anticipate when questions will be asked and are eager to participate. In our experience, students who recognize that they are actually engaged in meaningful learning rather than just memorizing, enjoy the endeavor, participate in the endeavor, and begin to ask why other instructors don't run their courses in the same way.

COURSE EVALUATIONS

Some instructors worry about how a change to an unfamiliar learning environment will impact student responses to course evaluations. This is a complex issue since most institutions' evaluation forms are designed as "customer satisfaction surveys" for the passive learning environment of the lecture hall.

If course evaluations by students are to have any meaning, they must "evaluate" all of the critical aspects of the course. Hence, recognizing the fact that learning is the responsibility of the student, course evaluations *must* include self-evaluation by the students.

Students' responses to any course, we believe, are related to the degree to which students' expectations for the course have been met. Thus, it is important that students' expectations for the course match your expectations for the course. This is another reason for establishing the "rules of the game" on the first meeting of the class and adhering to those rules in all aspects of the course. We discussed how this might be done in Chapter 7 when we considered ways of preparing students to participate in an active learning environment.

If course evaluations are an issue, it is important that the evaluations are consistent with the course design. If this is the case, and students have become active participants in the class, the evaluation forms will reflect the experiences of the students and will, in our experience, yield positive results. The key here, is to make sure that the evaluation form is consistent with your course design. The design of course evaluations, their applicability to the learning environment, and their misuse for administrative decisions were discussed in Chapter 13.

CRITICISM BY COLLEAGUES

Faculty are often concerned about the reactions of their colleagues to their attempts at creating an active learning environment. The concerns are multifaceted. Some feel that they will be criticized for not being "productive" in the classroom because they are not spending the majority of class time lecturing. The criticism stems from equating good teaching with good lecturing. When colleagues with this view visit a classroom in which group work is in progress, they view the room as being noisy and chaotic, reflecting an atmosphere in which significant learning cannot possibly take place. This view represents a misunderstanding of the learning process, and there is ample evidence in the literature to which these colleagues can be directed that support your attempt at creating an active learning environment. A good place to direct these colleagues as a starting point is a book recently published by the National Research Council entitled *How People Learn: Brain, Mind, Experience and School* (Bransford, et al., 1999).

Some faculty feel as if their colleagues will view them as "mavericks" if they attempt to deviate from the passive learning environment found in many classrooms, and, as a result, they will be ostracized. Others may feel pressure from faculty, who are comfortable with a passive learning environment, raising the point that students are passing their courses with high grades, so there is no need to change. For a variety of reasons related to local politics and personalities, this can be a valid concern. One way to approach the issue is to include the colleagues in your "experiment." Ask colleagues for suggestions about activities that they think could be beneficial in helping the learner to learn. Also, if the colleagues are involved in courses for which your course is a prerequisite, ask them for help in setting priorities for content topics in case there is not time to cover all of the topics previously covered in lecture. As for faculty who don't think they need to change, invite them to class so they can experience the difference between a passive and active learning environment.

FEAR

Some faculty express a fear of deviating from an established script in the classroom. They cite fear of losing control of the environment, and they cite fear of not being able to answer students' questions if they are not content "experts" in the subject that they are teaching.

Our advice to these faculty is to try engaging students in a limited way. Ease into the process. Although it is true that the instructor must have a level of specific content knowledge that is above that of a novice, it is not essential that he or she be a content "expert" and be able to address all questions that students might ask. The major contribution that an instructor can make in the student's learning is more related to process. In most cases, the instructor has more experience in organizing and integrating information into meaningful mental models. This is precisely the area in which most students need help.

If the instructor is to help the learner to learn, he or she must serve as a role model for students engaged in the learning process. Hence, it is not important that the instructor know all the answers, and acknowledging that you don't know it all sends an important message. What is important is that the instructor demonstrate how to engage in a process that leads to an appropriate answer. In many cases, the approach to an answer must begin from the view of the system that the student holds (i.e., the student's mental model). If a question is asked to which we do not have a "ready answer," we will often respond by saying, "I don't know the answer to your question, but let's see what makes sense." Another response might be, "I don't know, but let's see what the author of the text has to say about that." This process also helps us gain new insights into the material. This, in turn, leads to an understanding of the "content" at a higher level of complexity. We learn with the students. In addition, we gain confidence in the process, and, in a short time, the "fear factor," while maybe not gone, is certainly lessened.

IT'S JUST TOO HARD!

One objection that is commonly voiced is that making this change is just too hard. What this seems to mean is something like this. The time required to prepare for teaching in this way is too great. Or, the mental effort to teaching in this way is too great. Or, perhaps, the mental stress that would result from attempting such a fundamental change in how one teaches is too great.

We would never argue that change, and certainly not this change, *is easy*. The preparation time for anything new (a new course, lecture, laboratory) is always greater than the preparation time needed to do the same old thing once again. Thinking about new things, learning new things, is hard work. And yes, trying something new in front of a classroom full of students is scary and stressful.

But making the kind of change we are recommending does not take forever, and once accomplished, you will find yourself again in a new steady state with no more or less preparation time required and no more or less stress than occurred previously. Furthermore, learning something new can be exciting and stimulating, even when it does take hard work to accomplish. Finally, we argue that the change in student behavior and learning outcomes that will result from adopting the helping the learner to learn approach will be a reward that will make the hard work required worthwhile.

THE "REAL" OBSTACLE TO IMPLEMENTING
THE HELPING THE LEARNER TO LEARN MINDSET

The challenges that we have just discussed are among the most prevalent perceived by faculty attending our workshops. As workshop leaders, however, the biggest obstacle that we perceive to successfully implementing the helping the learner to learn mindset is reluctance on the part of instructors to adopt this mindset. Although these instructors intellectually recognize the implications of the mindset for learning, they hold on to the notion that their role in the process is to tell students things. This reluctance is not surprising. After all, experience with teachers throughout most of our educational careers, both as student and teacher, has been one of "give and receive." Teachers "give" knowledge, and students "receive" knowledge. Our role models in the classroom have operated under this premise, and this is what we have been trained to do.

Adopting a new mindset requires that we challenge our past experience. We must learn to trust the process, to believe that, given the opportunity and appropriate direction, the learner will learn. We must also recognize and accept that responsibility for learning lies with the learner. Our job is to help the learner with this process. To some, adopting the mindset implies that we must give up some control of the learning process. However, we never really had control over the student's learning—the student does. We can only control classroom activities, and this control is not lost by becoming a facilitator of the learning process.

So, the key to being successful is to focus on the learner. What is it that the student needs to be able to learn (i.e., reach the intended output state)? The answer to this question can only be achieved by asking a question (i.e, determining the input state), not by telling the student something. Once the instructor truly recognizes that this is the case, the process becomes clear, and helping the learner to learn becomes second nature.

A caveat is in order here. Adopting the helping the learner to learn mindset defines your path for interacting with students. It does not, *a priori*, mean that that path will provide a smooth ride. The process of determining what kind of help the learner needs and providing that help is often a difficult task that requires considerable reflection and work. However, in general, the rewards justify the effort. Each exchange with a student or group of students brings new insights, new food for thought, or new challenges to consider, and, sometimes, new frustrations. The boredom that often accompanies delivering lectures on the same topics year after year is not an issue. Although we may use the same words to convey information about a concept or to help students solve a problem in a given topic area, the motivation for doing so is often different. The "speech" is in response to a need voiced by the students. Because we learn as much, or sometimes more, from the students, each day in the classroom can be an exciting and fun experience.

We've considered what it means to help the learner to learn, how to use this mindset to direct classroom activities, how to get students to become active participants in the process, and how we can address a variety of challenges to the success of the process. We have, in essence, discussed the parameters defining the experiment. All that is left to do is run the experiment. However, this is always easier when the experiment, and its outcome, can be shared with colleagues. The next chapter discusses establishing a community in which this sharing can take place.

16

Building a Community
of Active Learning Practitioners

CHAPTER OVERVIEW

Teaching has traditionally been an activity that takes place behind the closed doors of one's classroom. However, success in transforming yourself into a creator of active learning environments is difficult if you stay isolated. Ideas will be proposed that can help to build an interactive community of active learning practitioners.

You've wanted to make some changes in the way you teach before but somehow never did. You think you'd like to try now. After all, you have lots of ideas after having read this far. However, it always seems easier to just do what you did last year; after all it clearly worked (almost all your students earned passing grades, and some of them really learned quite a lot). What do you do to actually start changing? What will you need to do to sustain any changes that you make in your learning environment?

Before providing some suggestions, let's see what it is about teaching as a profession that contributes to the problem of changing your approach to the classroom.

Teaching is a profession that, to a considerable extent, is carried out in isolation, behind the closed doors of a classroom with a group of students (large or small). Although you may discuss the course requirements for a major in geology or physics in a faculty meeting, it is much less common to talk with your colleagues about what you do when you are in the classroom. While you might discuss a case of cheating with a trusted senior colleague, it is less likely that you will discuss what method of student evaluation is most appropriate for your course objectives. While your students will evaluate your performance, your departmental colleagues have probably never observed you in the classroom, nor have you visited their classrooms.

TEACHING AS A SCHOLARLY ACTIVITY

Teaching has, traditionally, been very different from other aspects of academic life. Research and other forms of "scholarly work" are carried out in full view of other practitioners in the field. It is expected that you will learn from them and that what you learn will inform the work that you do. It is expected that you will critique what they do and that they will critique what you do. Scholarship, in all its forms, is a public activity that is carried out as a member of a community.

Does this contrast between teaching and other forms of scholarly work offer any clues about how to deal with the obstacles that seem to stand in the way of changing what you do in the classroom? We think it does. If you recognize that teaching, too, is a scholarly activity (Boyer, 1990), you will acknowledge the need to practice teaching in the same way that you practice any other scholarly activity.

In Chapter 14, we compared the behavior of *scientists in the laboratory* with the usual behavior of *science teachers in their classrooms*. We pointed out that every aspect of our description of how to help the learner to learn parallels the process of "doing" science. Now we need to extend that comparison to examine how we can make what we do in the classroom as public as what we do in the research laboratory.

BUILDING A COMMUNITY

The first step in transforming your teaching is to break out of the isolation of the classroom and begin to practice teaching as a part of a larger community of active learning practitioners. Recognize that, in many ways, the classroom is your laboratory. If you were involved in "bench science" research, you would seek out individuals from four broad communities with whom you could exchange ideas; a local community, a regional community, a national community, and an international community. One objective of that interaction would be to share the results from your research activities. If you adopt the helping the learner to learn mindset, and you become a reflective practitioner as we have suggested in Chapter 14, you have "data" to discuss with colleagues. If you think of the questions that arise regarding your classroom activities, the approaches that you take to answering those questions, and the response of the students to those approaches as reportable data (which it is), you have the basis for a "scholarly" exchange of ideas.

Begin with the local community. We often encounter the same faculty at a number of the workshops that we conduct in various regions of the country. One of the comments that these faculty make in their evaluation of the workshop is that it was good to see and interact with "old friends or colleagues" and become acquainted with "new people" who have common interests. These faculty are aware of each other, they know that they have common interests, and they recognize the value of such exchanges, but they fail to put a high enough priority on this activity to organize meetings expressly for reporting "results" of their educational activities, peer review of their educational efforts, and sharing ideas for future "experiments." In fact, it is this type of exchange that provides reconfirmation of, and support for, what you do, stimulates ideas for trying new approaches to solving the problems that you encounter, and keeps the endeavor fun. Because the focus is on helping the learner to learn, the members of these local groups need not necessarily be from your discipline or even from science disciplines. The general issues related to how students learn and the challenges that they face in trying to learn are not restricted to specific disciplines. Certainly, there are issues that are discipline-related, and these are better discussed among members of the same discipline, but colleagues from other areas can still provide considerable help for these issues.

Start with colleagues in your department or college (including adjunct faculty). Look for colleagues at neighboring educational institutions. Look for local sections of national organizations (see further). Share ideas if nothing else. Even better, go into each others' classrooms, and see what other people do and how they do it. Invite colleagues to see what you do. Talk about teaching within the widest possible community of practitioners.

Look to your professional organizations (the American Chemical Society and its section on Chemical Education, the American Association of Physics Teachers, National Association of Biology Teachers; there are many others) and to interdisciplinary organizations (American Educational Research Association, the National Association for Research on Science Teaching). They have meetings and workshops, and publish journals (or sections of journals) devoted to teaching issues. Some have websites with areas designed to foster communication among faculty. Attend the meetings, participate in the workshops, and read the journals. Find out what others are doing in their teaching. You will be amazed that many of the issues that you have thought about within the confines of your office are issues that others have and are thinking about with respect to their educational efforts.

You have something to offer them, and, we believe, it is your obligation as a member of the academic community to share your experience and insights with the community at large. Contribute your experiences and thoughts about teaching your discipline to the conversations that occur (in person or in the literature).

The bottom line is if you adopt the helping the learner to learn mindset, you become a part of a community of educators whose goal is to improve the educational process, not just disseminate information about a particular content area. By recognizing that you are part of such a community, you should also recognize that you have an obligation to participate in that community and that you can derive benefit from that community. In other words, pursue professional expertise in *teaching science* in the same way that you would pursue expertise in *doing science*. In answer to the question that has just come to mind, "Yes, there are funding sources that support projects aimed at improving the process of learning science."

17

The Bottom Line

You've read this far, and now you are probably thinking, "Okay, so what is the bottom line, take-home message, and, if I 'buy' it, what is my next step?"

The bottom line is that we want our students to engage in meaningful learning. This means that they must recognize that they must take responsibility for their learning, and that the key to meaningful learning is the process of building, testing, and refining mental models. It is our job, as teachers, to help them become active participants in this process and to help them become proficient at engaging in this process.

To accomplish this, we must set appropriate goals for their learning; goals aimed at using information to "solve" problems. We must also interact with the learners to assess their current knowledge base and their skills in applying that knowledge. Knowing where they are (their input state) and what we want them to be able to do (the output state), we can help them "chart their course" by providing appropriate learning experiences that will help them test and refine their mental models.

We also must help them recognize conceptual and reasoning errors when they occur so that they can make appropriate modifications to their mental models. To do this, we must be diagnosticians, and, in this role, we must probe students' mental models in an attempt to discover where and why difficulties may be occurring.

Finally, we must be reflective practitioners. We must reflect on what went on in the classroom, on the answers that students offered in response to our questions, on the explanations that students offered to explain various phenomena, and on our interactions with students.

In this book, we have tried to provide you with a foundation for approaching this bottom line. We have raised what we believe are the critical issues, and we have shared our views on those issues. Can you be successful at helping the learner to learn if you don't create your learning environment in the same way that we do? Of course you can. You must be comfortable (and safe) in the learning environment, and you must use the tools that best suit you to achieve the goal of helping the learner to learn.

So, what is your next (or first) step if you want to implement the "helping the learner to learn" mindset? Perhaps the most difficult step in this process is moving from an intellectual understanding of the goal to adopting the principle as a governing philosophy that directs your actions as an educator. Our suggestion for approaching this transition is to continue to do whatever it is that you do in the classroom. Begin by becoming a reflective practitioner. When you are done with class, ask yourself, "What were my output state goals for the day?" and "Did I help the learner to learn today?" If the answer is "no," think about what you could have done differently to help the learner to learn. If the answer is "yes," think about how you know this. It is not sufficient to think, "Well, they seemed to follow the material, and they didn't ask questions, so they must have learned." You must have acquired evidence during the class that the students, in fact, learned something and at least approached the output state goals for the day.

Our prediction is that, after engaging in this type of reflection, you will want to try something in the classroom that will help the students achieve your output state goals for the day. Go ahead and try it. It need not be a complete change in what you do in the classroom. It can be a small experiment to see if the prediction that you made in your office was correct. At this point, you are on your way. As in any new endeavor, take one step at a time, and don't be afraid to make mistakes. As a reflective practitioner, you will learn from the mistakes as well as the successes.

Have fun!

REFERENCES

Alkin, M. C. (Ed.). (1992). *Encyclopedia of educational research* (6th ed.). New York: Macmillan Publishing, Inc.

Allen, D. E. (1997). Bringing problem-based learning to the introductory biology classroom. In A. P. McNeal & C. D'Avanzo (Eds.), *Student-active science: Models of innovation in college science teaching* (pp. 259–275). Fort Worth, TX: Saunders College Publishing.

Angelo, T. A. (1993). Classroom assessment: Assessing to improve higher learning in the life sciences. *Annals of the New York Academy of Sciences, 701,* 61–75.

Angelo, T. A., & Cross, K. P. (1993). *Classroom assessment techniques: A handbook for college teachers* (2nd ed.). San Francisco: Jossey-Bass.

Appleton, K. (1997). Analysis and description of students' learning during science classes using a constructivist-based model. *Journal of Research in Science Teaching, 34,* 303–318.

Aronson, E., & Patnoe, S. (1997). *The jigsaw classroom: Building cooperation in the classroom* (2nd ed.). New York: Addison Wesley Longman.

Bagno, E., & Eylon, B. S. (1997). From problem solving to a knowledge structure: an example from the domain of electromagnetism. *American Journal of Physics, 65,* 726–736.

Barrows, H. S. (1983). Problem-based, self-directed learning. *Journal of the American Medical Association, 250,* 3077–3080.

Bloom, B. S. (Ed.). (1956). *Taxonomy of educational objectives, Handbook I: Cognitive domain.* New York: David McKay Company, Inc.

Blumenfeld, P. C., Marx, R. W., Soloway, E., & Krzjcik, J. (1996). Learning with peers: from small group cooperation to collaborative communities. *Educational Researcher, 25*(8), 37–40.

Bossert, S. T. (1988). Cooperative activities in the classroom. *Review of Research in Education, 15,* 225–250.

Bosworth, K., & Hamilton, S. J. (Eds.). (1994). *Collaborative learning: Underlying processes and effective techniques.* San Francisco: Jossey-Bass.

Boud, D., & Feletti, G. E. (Eds.). (1997). *The challenge of problem-based learning* (2nd ed.). London: Kogan Page.

Boyer, E. L. (1990). *Scholarship reconsidered: Priorities of the professoriate.* Princeton, NJ: The Carnegie Foundation for the Advancement of Teaching.

Bransford, J. D., Brown, A. L., & Cocking, R. R. (Eds.). (1999). *How people learn: Brain, mind, experience, and school.* Washington, DC: National Academy Press.

Brown, A. L., & Palincsar, A. S. (1989). Guided, cooperative learning and individual knowledge acquisition. In L. B. Resnick (Ed.), *Knowing, learning, and instruction: Essays in honor of Robert Glaser* (pp. 393–451). Hillsdale, NJ: Lawrence Erlbaum Associates.

Brown, A. M., & Stubbs, D. W. (Eds.). (1983). *Medical physiology.* New York: John Wiley and Sons.

Brown, T. L., LeMay, H. E., Jr., & Bursten, B. E. (2000). *Chemistry: The central science* (8th ed.). Upper Saddle River, NJ: Prentice Hall.

Bunce, D. M., Gabel, D. L., & Samuel, J. V. (1991). Enhancing chemistry problem-solving achievement using problem categorization. *Journal of Research in Science Teaching, 28,* 505–521.

Campbell, N. A., Reece, J. B., & Mitchell, L. G. (1999). *Biology* (5th ed.). Menlo Park, CA: Benjamin/Cummings.

Chi, M. T. H., De Leeuw, N., Chiu, M. H., & LaVancher, C. (1994). Eliciting self-explanations improves understanding. *Cognitive Science, 18,* 439–477.

Chi, M. T. H., & vanLehn, K. A. (1991). The content of physics self-explanations. *Journal of the Learning Sciences, 1,* 69–105.

Cooper, M. A. (1999). Classroom choices from a cognitive perspective on peer learning. In A. M. O'Donnell & A. King (Eds.), *Cognitive perspectives on peer learning* (pp. 215–233). Mahwah, NJ: Lawrence Erlbaum Associates.

D'Avanzo, C., & McNeal, A. P. (1997). Research for all students: Structuring investigation into first-year courses. In A. P. McNeal & C. D'Avanzo (Eds.), *Student-active science: Models of innovation in college science teaching* (pp. 279–299). Houston, TX: Saunders College Publishing.

Davis, M. H., & Harden, R. M. (1999). AMEE Medical Education Guide No. 15: Problem-based learning: A practical guide. *Medical Teacher, 21,* 130–140.

Derry, S. J. (1999). A fish called peer learning: Searching for common themes. In A. M. O'Donnell & A. King (Eds.), *Cognitive perspectives on peer learning* (pp. 197–211). Mahwah, NJ: Lawrence Erlbaum Associates.

Dinan, F. J., & Frydrychowski, V. A. (1995). A team learning method for organic chemistry. *Journal of Chemical Education, 72,* 429–431.

Doran, R. L., Lawrenz, F., & Helgeson, S. (1994). Research on assessment in science. In D. L. Gabel (Ed.), *Handbook of research on science teaching and learning* (pp. 388–442). New York: Macmillan Publishing Company.

Dougherty, R. C., Bowen, C. W., Berger, T., Rees, W., Melton, E. K., & Pullam, E. (1995). Cooperative learning and enhanced communications. *Journal of Chemical Education, 72,* 793–797.

Frawley, W. (1988). Relational models and metascience. In M. Evens (Ed.), *Relational models of the lexicon* (pp. 297–333). Cambridge, UK: Cambridge University Press.

Gillespie, R. J., Humphreys, D. A., Baird, N. C., & Robinson, E. A. (1986). *Chemistry.* Boston: Allyn and Bacon, Inc.

Goodsell, A., Maher, M., & Tinto, V. (1992). *Collaborative learning: A sourcebook for higher education.* University Park, PA: National Center for Postsecondary Teaching, Learning, and Assessment.

Halpern, D. F. (1996). *Thought and knowledge: An introduction to critical thinking* (3rd ed.). Mahwah, NJ: Lawrence Erlbaum Associates.

Heller, P., & Hollabaugh, M. (1992). Teaching problem solving through cooperative grouping. Part 2: Designing problems and structuring groups. *American Journal of Physics, 60,* 637–644.

Heller, P., Keith, R., & Anderson, S. (1992). Teaching problem solving through cooperative grouping. Part 1: Group versus individual problem solving. *American Journal of Physics, 60,* 627–636.

Herbert, D. (1965). *Mr. Wizard's science secrets.* New York: Hawthorn Books, Inc.

Jensen, M. S., & Finley, F. N. (1996). Changes in students' understanding of evolution resulting from different curricular and instructional strategies. *Journal of Research in Science Teaching, 33,* 879–900.

Johnson, D. W., Johnson, R. T., & Smith, K. A. (1998). *Active learning: Cooperation in the college classroom.* Edina, MN: Interaction Book Co.

Johnson, G. B., & Raven, P. H. (1996). *Biology: Principles & explorations.* Austin, TX: Holt, Rinehart and Winston.

Kagan, S., & Kagan, M. (1994). The structural approach: Six keys to cooperative learning. In S. Sharan (Ed.), *Handbook of cooperative learning methods* (pp. 115–133). Westport, CT: Greenwood Press.

Larkin, J. H. (1985). Understanding, problem representations, and skill in physics. In S. F. Chipman, J. W. Segal, & Glaser, R. (Eds.), *Thinking and learning skills, Vol 2: Research and open questions* (pp. 141–159). Hillsdale, NJ: Lawrence Erlbaum Associates.

Lemke, J. L. (1990). *Talking science: Language, learning and values.* Norwood, NJ: Ablex Publishing.

Leonard, W. J., Dufresne, R. J., & Mestre, J. (1996). Using qualitative problem-solving strategies to highlight the role of conceptual knowledge in solving problems. *American Journal of Physics, 64,* 1495–1503.

Lesgold, A. (1988). Problem solving. In R. J. Sternberg & E. E. Smith (Eds.), *The psychology of human thought* (pp. 188–213). Cambridge, UK: Cambridge University Press.

Lumpe, A. T., & Staver, J. R. (1995). Peer collaboration and concept development: Learning about photosynthesis. *Journal of Research in Science Teaching, 32,* 71–98.

Lunetta, V. N. (1990). Cooperative learning in science, mathematics, and computer problem solving. In M. Gardner, J. G. Greeno, F. Reif, A. H. Schoenfeld, A. diSessa, & E. Stage (Eds.), *Towards a scientific practice of science education* (pp. 235–249). Hillsdale, NJ: Lawrence Erlbaum Associates.

Macbeth, D. (2000). On an actual apparatus for conceptual change. *Science Education, 84,* 228–264.

Mazur, E. (1997). *Peer instruction.* Upper Saddle River, NJ: Prentice Hall.

McDermott, L. C. (1991). What we teach and what is learned—closing the gap. *American Journal of Physics, 59,* 301–315.

Meirson, S. (1998). A problem-based learning course in physiology for undergraduate and graduate basic science students. *American Journal of Physiology, 275 (Advances in Physiology Education, 20),* S16–27.

Michael, J. A. (1993). Teaching problem solving in small groups. *Annals of the New York Academy of Sciences, 701,* 37–48.

Michael, J. A. (1998). Students' misconceptions about perceived physiological responses. *American Journal of Physiology, 274 (Advances in Physiology Education, 19),* S90–S98.

Michael, J. A., & Rovick, A. A. (1999). *Problem solving in physiology.* Upper Saddle River, NJ: Prentice-Hall, Inc.

Michael, J. A., Richardson, D., Rovick, A., Modell, H., Bruce, D., Horwitz, B., Hudson, M., Silverthorn, D., Whitescarver, S., & Williams, S. (1999). Undergraduate students' misconceptions about respiratory physiology. *American Journal of Physiology, 277 (Advances in Physiology Education, 22),* S127–S135.

Michael, J. A., Wenderoth, M. P., Modell, H. I., Cliff, W., Horwitz, B., McHale, P., Richardson, D., Silverthorn, D., Williams, S., & Whitescarver, S. (2002). Undergraduates' understanding of cardiovascular phenomena. *Advances in Physiology Education, 26,* 72–84.

Mintzes, J. J., Wandersee, J. H., & Novak, J. D. (Eds.). (2000). *Assessing science understanding: A human constructivist view.* San Diego, CA: Academic Press.

Modell, H. (1992). A mechanism for evaluating our teaching efforts. *FASEB Journal 6,* A1521.

Modell, H. I. (1991). Designing protocols for student laboratories. *Computers in Life Science Education, 8,* 91–94.

Modell, H. I., & Carroll, R. G. (1993). Promoting active learning in large groups. *Annals of the New York Academy of Sciences, 701,* 49–60.

Modell, H. I., Michael, J. A., Adamson, T., Goldberg, J., Horwitz, B. A., Bruce, D. S., Hudson, M. L., Whitescarver, S. A., & Williams, S. (2000). Helping undergraduates repair faulty mental models in the student laboratory. *Advances in Physiology Education, 23,* 82–90.

Norman, D. A. (1980). Cognitive engineering and education. In D. T. Tuma & F. Reif (Eds.), *Problem solving and education: Issues in teaching and research* (pp. 97–110). Hillsdale, NJ: Lawrence Erlbaum Associates.

Novak, J. D. (1998). *Learning, creating, and using knowledge: Concept maps (TM) as facilitative tools in school and corporations.* Mahwah, NJ: Lawrence Erlbaum Associates.

Novak, J. D., & Gowin, D. B. (1984). *Learning how to learn.* Cambridge, UK: Cambridge University Press.

Ploger, D. (1988). Reasoning and the structure of knowledge in biochemistry. *Instructional Science, 17,* 57–76.

Qin, Z., Johnson, D. W., & Johnson, R. T. (1995). Cooperative versus competitive efforts and problem solving. *Review of Educational Research, 65,* 129–143.

Rangachari, P. K. (1991). Design of a problem-based undergraduate course in pharmacology: Implications for the teaching of physiology. *American Journal of Physiology, 260 (Advances in Physiology Education, 5)*: S14–S21.

Reif, F. (1985). Acquiring an effective understanding of scientific concepts. In L. H. T. West & A. L. Pines (Eds.), *Cognitive structure and conceptual change* (pp. 133–151). Orlando, FL: Academic Press.

Rovick, A. A., & Michael, J. A. (1992). The predictions table: A tool for assessing students' knowledge. *American Journal of Physiology, 263 (Advances in Physiology Education, 8)*: S33–S36.

Rovick, A. A., Michael, J. A., Modell, H. I., Bruce, D. A. Horwitz, B., Adamson, T., Richardson, D. R., Silverthorn, D. U., & Whitescarver, S. A. (1999). How accurate are our assumptions about our students' background knowledge? *American Journal of Physiology, 276 (Advances in Physiology Education, 21)*: S93–S101.

Rowe, M. (1974). Relation of wait-time and rewards to the development of language, logic and fate control: A. Part One: wait time. *Journal of Research in Science Teaching, 11,* 81–94.

Sadler, P. M. (1998). Psychometric models of student conceptions in science: Reconciling qualitative studies and distractor-driven assessment instruments. *Journal of Research in Science Teaching, 35,* 265–296.

Schön, D. A. (1983). *The reflective practitioner.* New York: Basic Books.

Seeley, R. R., Stephens, T. D., & Tate, P. (Eds). (2000). *Anatomy and physiology* (5th ed.). Boston, MA: McGraw-Hill.

Segal, J. W., Chipman, S. F., & Glaser, R. (Eds). (1985). *Thinking and learning skills, Vol. 1: Relating instruction to research.* Hillsdale, NJ: Lawrence Erlbaum Associates.

Shafritz, J. M., Koeppe, R. P., & Soper, E. W. (1988). *The facts on file dictionary of education.* New York: Facts on File.

Silverthorn, D. U. (2001). *Human physiology: An integrative approach* (2nd ed.). Upper Saddle River, NJ: Prentice Hall.

Simon, H. (1999). Problem solving. In R. A. Wilson & F. C. Keil (Eds.), *The MIT encyclopedia of the cognitive sciences* (pp. 674–676). Cambridge, MA: The MIT Press.

Smith, E. L. (1991). A conceptual change model of learning science. In S. M. Glynn, R. H. Yeany, & B. K. Britton (Eds.), *The psychology of learning science* (pp. 43–63). Hillsdale, NJ: Lawrence Erlbaum Associates.

Spiro, R. J., Feltovich, P. J., Coulson, R. L., & Anderson, D. K. (1989). Multiple analogies for complex concepts: Antidotes for analogy induced misconceptions in advanced knowledge acquisition. In S. Vosniadou & A. Ortony (Eds.), *Similarity and analogical reasoning* (pp. 498–531). Cambridge, UK: Cambridge University Press.

Stewart, J., & Hafner, R. (1994). Research on problem solving: Genetics. In D. L. Gabel (Ed.), *Handbook of research on science teaching and learning* (pp. 284–300). New York: Macmillan Publishing Company.

Tarbuck, E. J., & Lutgens, F. K. (2000). *Earth science* (9th ed.). Upper Saddle River, NJ: Prentice Hall.

Tobin, K., & Capie, W. (1980). The effects of teacher wait time and questioning quality on middle school science achievement. *Journal of Research in Science Teaching, 17,* 469–475.

Torp, L., & Sage, S. (1998). *Problems as possibilities: Problem-based learning for K–12 education.* Alexandria, VA: Association for Supervision and Curriculum Development.

Tortora, G. J., & Funke, B. R. (1997). *Microbiology: An introduction* (6th ed.). Menlo Park, CA: Addison Wesley Longman, Inc.

Tsaparlis. G., & Angelopoulos, V. (2000). A model of problem solving: Its operation, validity, and usefulness in the case of organic-synthesis problems. *Science Education, 84,* 131–153.

Wandersee, J. H., Mintzes, J. J., & Novak, J. D. (1994). Research on alternative conceptions in science. In D. L. Gabel (Ed.), *Handbook of research on science teaching and learning* (pp. 177–210). New York: Macmillan Publishing.

Watson, S. B. (1992). The essential elements of cooperative learning. *American Biology Teacher, 54,* 84–86.

Williams, S. (1992). Putting case-based instruction in context: Examples from legal and medical education. *Journal of the Learning Sciences, 2,* 367–427.

Wu, H. K., Krajcik, J. S., & Soloway, E. (2001). Promoting understanding of chemical representations: Students' use of a visualization tool in the classroom. *Journal of Research in Science Teaching, 38,* 821–842.

Zeichner, K. M., & Liston, D. P. (1996). *Reflective teaching: An introduction.* Mahwah, NJ: Lawrence Erlbaum Associates.

AUTHOR INDEX

165

SUBJECT INDEX

A

Active learning environment,17, 53, 58-59,
    63-75, 78, 79-81, 83-84, 87,
    89-96, 97-104, 105-113,
    131-132, 144-148
  definition, 6
Analogies, use of, 12, 44
Assessment, 12, 32-33, 42, 43-51, 67, 96,
    109
  classroom, 67, 128-129
  course, 50
  input state, 31-33, 51
  pre-test/post-test, 129
  student, 96, 117-126
  tests, 117-126

B

Building a community, 153-156

C

Cases, use of, 22, 55, 110-111, 125
CD-ROM, use of, 85-86
Clarification, students seeking, 48, 66,
    68-74, 104
Computers, uses of, 85-87
Concept mapping, 13, 118, 125
Conceptual change, 5

Conference room, 89-96, 104, 109
Constructivism, 4-5, 9-11, 14-15, 18
Course content, 124, 144-145
Course evaluation, 127-135, 147
Course objectives, 113, 117-118, 128, 153

D

Diagnosing misconceptions, 46-48, 57
Dialogue, 56, 57, 67, 73-74
Discussion section, 25, 48, 57, 89-96
Diversity, classroom, 44, 65
Diversity of interpretation, 69-70, 70, 73

E

Educational experience, 14, 27, 31, 37, 81.
    See also Learning experience
Educational objectives, 38-39, 89-91,
    117-118. *See also* Output state
Expectations for student learning, 33,
    40-42, 112, 117, 132, 146. *See
    also* Goals and *also* Objectives
Explanation (as a sign of understanding),
    3, 9, 10, 17-18, 19, 21, 22, 25,
    26, 56-57, 81, 121-122

F

Facilitator, 66, 77, 105, 110-112, 124